Gershon

Be a fox!

Chantell Ilbury / Clem Sunter

The Mind of a
FOX

Scenario Planning in *Action*

HUMAN & ROUSSEAU / TAFELBERG

Published jointly by Human & Rousseau
and Tafelberg Publishers,
both 28 Wale Street, Cape Town
© 2001 Human & Rousseau
and Tafelberg Publishers

Designed by Jürgen Fomm
and typeset in 11.5 on 14 pt Palatino
Printed and bound by
Paarl Print, Oosterland Street, Paarl,
South Africa

First edition, first impression June 2001
Second impression August 2001
Third impression October 2001
Fourth impression February 2002
Fifth impression May 2002
Sixth impression June 2002
Seventh impression August 2002

ISBN 0 7981 4169 7

THIS BOOK IS DEDICATED TO

Our families who are our foundation;
Our friends who stand by us in good
  and bad times;
Our colleagues who assisted us in producing
  the book in such a professional manner;
  and
The fox within you – whoever you are,
  wherever you are and whatever you do.

The fox knows many things – the hedgehog one big one.
ARCHILOCUS, c. 650 B. C.

A fox once saw a crow with a piece of cheese in her beak.
He was hungry, so he resolved to acquire it for himself.
"What a beautiful bird you are," he cried, "I am sure you
must have a beautiful voice to match your body. Will
you not sing to me?" The crow was flattered. She opened
her beak and gave a harsh croak. Down fell the cheese,
whereupon the fox pounced upon it and ate it.
AESOP'S FABLES, c. 620 B. C.

Introduction to the Third Impression

We normally associate 911 with an emergency call. It also represents September 11. At 8:45 am (New York time) on that day in 2001, the world changed forever. This was the moment when the first of two hijacked planes slammed into the World Trade Center. Another one hit the Pentagon and a fourth crashed in Pennsylvania. No terrorist attack has ever caused such a shock. The *unthinkable* had happened – and it wasn't a movie.

When we wrote this book in the first part of 2001, we included a letter to President Bush. In it, we warned him that the key uncertainty during his tenure was nuclear terrorism, more specifically the possibility of terrorists planting a nuclear device in a Western city. While the tools of destruction and method of delivery were different to what we had envisaged, the impact was just as devastating. Nothing could have demonstrated the power of scenario planning more effectively than this terrible tragedy. We could never have captured it in a forecast, but it was possible to provide a warning in the form of a scenario.

Indeed, the logic contained in our two scenarios – "Friendly Planet" and "Gilded Cage" – is now more pertinent than ever. The natural temptation for the "rich old millions" in the West must be to batten down the hatches and isolate themselves in a Gilded Cage. We all know that security is the most basic of all human needs. However, this could lead to an even more divided world as the gap between the "rich old millions" and the "poor young billions" widens further. The increasing tension and stress associated with this scenario will ironically make it more likely than before that another evil act of the same – or perhaps even greater – magnitude will be perpetrated by terrorists. No advances in technology, no improvements in intelligence and security management systems can render an individual nation impregnable against attack. The terrorist will always find a chink in the bars of the cage, however thick you make them, to pass through and commit his foul deed. Moreover, the knowledge of how to manufacture weapons of mass destruction is itself indestructible. And it will continue to spread. Meanwhile, inside the cage, a superabundance of soft targets awaits the terrorist. The growing interdependencies and networks of a modern society make it increasingly vulnerable to dislocation and attack, particularly by people who are prepared to die in the process.

The only way to minimise – not entirely eliminate – the threat of further outrages is for America to take the lead in building a Friendly Planet. This involves more than a military victory over the terrorists. The realisation has to dawn that to be a secure winner, you cannot be surrounded by resentful losers. The preferred scenario is therefore one in which, as we say in the book, "the rich old millions resolve to find common ground with the poor young billions to eradicate poverty and disease, to tackle problems of the environment, to bring international criminal syndicates to justice and to root out dangerous terrorist organisations." Otherwise, the future is bleak. Anything goes. And it would be unwise to dismiss *any* 911 call as a hoax.

Chantell Ilbury
Clem Sunter
September 2001

Eye of the tiger or fox of the fairway?

Have you ever watched the world's finest golfer blast the ball effortlessly from a tee, then follow his crisp iron shot at the pin with a perfect putt and think "he really needs to jack up his game"? Of course you don't, but he does, even when he is about to win the 2001 Masters and have all four Major trophies sitting on his mantelpiece at the same time. This is Tiger Woods – the fox of the fairway. Why a fox? He is cunning, bright, curious and he reacts with his environment. The *New York Times* once described foxes as "the most beautiful and interesting animals to observe".

The common fox in Europe has reddish fur with black patches behind the ears and a light tip to its brush-like tail. Underneath, it sports a white waistcoat and dark leggings. Including the tail, the animal is just over a metre long. It is a small but beautiful wild dog, the eyes having a watchful gleam quite different to a domesticated dog. The whole demeanour of the animal is one of alertness, as if it would be up and off at the first sign of danger.

Beautiful – yes; but interesting? Foxes have many dens, sometimes called earths, within their territory. They use them to their best advantage because dens give them options. Foxes normally choose the most secure den in which to give birth to and nurture their young, but they maintain the other dens in case the secure one is put at risk. They are continually foraging for new sources of food and eat almost anything – rodents, rabbits, birds and insects as well as fruit and berries in season. They are highly adaptable to different terrains, ranging from dense forests to cultivated farmland. In fact, they can adapt easily to urban environments and change their eating habits accordingly. Scavenging from refuse bins is an urban pastime. They are so resourceful that the landed gentry in England find them fun to hunt; but maybe not for much longer if the politicians have their way. Foxes have extraordinarily sensitive noses that can pick up an interesting scent a mile off. Even the spiky exterior of the humble hedgehog can't protect it from a hungry fox.

Which brings us to hedgehogs. They, on the other hand, live in one burrow all their lives. For them a single home is their security – nice and warm and cosy, and generally quite big. Hedgehogs hibernate during winter, effectively cutting themselves off from the outside world. They have plump little bodies with very short legs that hardly raise them from the ground. They are all of thirty centimetres long, covered with sharp, greyish brown spikes and blessed with a pig-like snout. Unlike foxes, hedgehogs like to live where there is certainty in the availability of food. Their favourite fare includes insects, but they are also partial to snails and slugs, which are slow enough for them to catch. Hedgehogs are generally non-confrontational. Whereas foxes will readily enter a fight, hedgehogs prefer to roll up in a ball and use their protective spikes to deter any challenge, especially from foxes. Nevertheless, foxes are carnivorous and are not unknown to make a tasty meal of sleepy hedgehogs. And gypsies have been known to bake them in a covering of clay.

Foxes? Hedgehogs? What have these got to do with golf? And more importantly, what can we learn from distinguishing between them? This book attempts to uncover the mind of a fox. What makes someone a fox? How does a fox manoeuvre not only through the game of business, but also through the game of life? In order to gain an insight into the versatile mind of the fox, we need to compare it to the stiffer persona of the staid hedgehog.

In brief, a hedgehog is a person who believes that life revolves around one big idea, one ultimate truth and that if only we can get at that idea or truth, everything else will come right. Once programmed or hooked on an idea, or even worse an ideology, a hedgehog cannot shake it off. Alternatives are irrelevant. As opposed to searching for a hypothesis which most closely fits the facts, a hedgehog will shoehorn the facts into something which will support his ideology, however much the arguments have to be distorted.

A fox, in contrast to a hedgehog, is someone who believes that life is all about knowing many things. Foxes are people who embrace uncertainty and believe that experience – doing things – is an essential source of knowledge. Action sorts out the sheep from the goats! Moreover, like good golfers know that an excellent sub-par round is only built up one shot at a time, foxes depend upon an incremental approach to change the status quo. Life very rarely confronts you with life-changing experiences. Rather, the transformation of your prospects is the result of many small steps taken one at a time, with little knowledge in advance of what the next step will be until it presents itself. Hence, foxes understand that it is a waste of time trying to delineate an exact path into the long-term future. Crossroads upon crossroads upon crossroads await you. You take the turning you like at the time, and you never look over your shoulder. Consequently, while hedgehogs like to bury themselves in certainty and cloister themselves from disruptive influences, foxes enthusiastically forage for new ideas and explore new routes in the quest of developing a wider range of options for nourishment. In pursuing this course, foxes rely as much on intuition and imagination as they do on their reason and senses. James Dyson, a well-known and very foxy British inventor, puts his success down to his obsession for detail and never-say-die approach to problem-solving: "Once you begin to break down a problem into little bits and tackle each one you find a solution." Voilà – he has completely redesigned the vacuum cleaner, the wheelbarrow and the washing machine and is worth £500 million.

Returning to the world of golf, how would a hedgehog-like golfer differ from Tiger Woods? Firstly, he would have a pre-tournament press conference at which he would expand at great length on his vision and strategic plan for the event. If conditions during the tournament were exactly as predicted in his plan and he played the course exactly as he had anticipated, he might win it. But if the weather was different, the course tougher, and things did not go according to plan, he would end up with a series of lousy scores and his name way down the list. He might even call a post-tournament conference to complain how things totally beyond his control had led to his demise: for example, the state of the greens, the newness of his clubs or the unruly nature of the spectators. Hedgehogs can be bad losers cum laude!

Resilience is where Tiger has such an advantage over his fellow competitors, and permits him to win by such large margins in tournaments. For the reality is that things seldom go according to plan for any player, however consistent he is; and Tiger is more consistent than most. Where Tiger puts clear blue water between himself and the rest of the field is his ability to turn adversity into opportunity. When he hits a wayward shot, his powers of recovery are sublime. If his drive ends up behind a tree, he can hook or slice his iron shot so that the ball bends in flight and lands on the green. From "unplayable" lies just off the putting surface, he invents a chip shot which leaves his ball centimetres from the hole. He holes long putts when he needs to. He can stop a shot in mid-swing when he hears the inopportune click of a spectator's camera shutter.

Tiger has the strength, the touch and the imagination to be the champion. In addition, he possesses the vital characteristic of BMT or big match temperament. None of these qualities is spontaneously acquired. Admittedly, in Tiger's case, he always had the potential; his father spotted it at the age of three. However, his current prowess has arisen from years of preparation, hard physical training and focus. He can make those minor adjustments to his game which are crucial to his victories precisely because, more than any other mortal on earth, he has achieved mastery over what he can control – his shot-making. He has the flexibility because he has the focus. This may sound contradictory! Nevertheless, we are going to show you later in the book that focusing one's energy is a prerequisite for the capacity to manoeuvre out of difficult situations.

Two boardroom species

As in golf, so in business there are plenty of hedgehog CEOs. Some achieve spectacular results in terms of earnings-per-share growth and capital appreciation for shareholders. But their companies have invariably been fortunate enough to experience business conditions in line with their own wishes or reflecting the assumptions contained in their strategic plans. It is only when the future branches off in an unexpected and undesired direction that the mettle of a CEO is tested and you can tell whether he is a fox or a hedgehog.

An obvious indicator of a hedgehog CEO is that he shoots the equivalent of a golf score in the upper 90s when he experiences the unexpected. Then he explains in the annual report and to members at the annual general meeting how the mess is due to adverse factors beyond his control; but the company is doing something about it! When things go badly on the golf course, cheating hedgehogs have been known to move their balls surreptitiously to better lies by employing the "foot wedge" – another name for an adroit little kick. The other tactic is to replace the ball nearer the hole on the green after cleaning it. In competition, hedgehog "ringers" might even enter a better score on their cards than they actually achieved; or bolster their handicaps beforehand by logging in artificially high scores. In business, the hedgehog equivalent is to use strong-arm tactics to retain market share, be unmerciful towards suppliers, bully the employees or subtly embroider the accounts. In the short term, hedgehogs have lots of ways of covering up bad track records! The amazing thing is that hedgehog CEOs can still come out smelling like roses and pay themselves huge bonuses with the full support of the board's remuneration committee. A recent UK study showed that there is no correlation whatsoever between CEOs' pay and performance.

On the other hand, Tiger Woods has to perform within the rules to be paid. If he didn't regularly shoot rounds in the 60s, if his name wasn't regularly at the top of the leader board, he wouldn't get the sponsorship fees or prize money. Tiger cannot bamboozle anyone with fine statements of intent about strategic restructuring or repositioning. His clubs do the talking and the results speak for themselves!

The examples chosen from golf and business highlight how different a hedgehog is from a fox. Hedgehogs are inflexible and slow to move. However, once they start on a course, they don't deviate. Inertia sets in. Because so many hedgehogs in the animal kingdom have been flattened by cars, they now have their own tunnels excavated for them under motorways by caring preservation societies. Colin Powell, the American secretary of state who was previously an army man, makes it clear in his autobiography that he despises military people in the hedgehog mould. They are immaculately dressed but make little practical contribution. According to Powell, all they do is "break starch", namely put on trousers that have been starched to perfection. In other words, hedgehogs are conspicuous at military parades, bristling with importance and marching to the thump of the big bass drum. But they are seldom seen in the trenches doing the actual fighting and showing courage under fire.

By contrast, foxes are quick to make changes in their actual behaviour. Occasionally, these are large changes, as when Reynard the fox leaps out of the chicken coop when he sees Farmer Giles coming out of the farmhouse door with his shotgun! Their intuitive response is what allows them to survive in a changing environment. One point which is constantly missed by management text books and business school courses is that 80 per cent of the success of world-class companies is due to excellence in implementation and delivery under a variety of conditions. They are simply brilliant at reaching their goals even when things crop up which they were not registering on their radar screens. At the most, 20 per cent of their success is attributable to the quality of their original plans or the conceptual part of the management process that the majority of management gurus write big tomes about. In the real world, the adaptations along the way are the ones that count. The trick is not the inventive idea: discoveries which will set the world alight are a dime a dozen. The trick is co-ordinating the 101 little things that make the idea happen. Think of the percentage of boardroom decisions that never get further than the minute book.

World-class companies tend therefore to be run by foxy CEOs who are not obsessed with the "vision" thing. They are

15

prepared to contemplate views that are contrary to their company's conventional wisdom and "official future". They seek to attract people who are lateral thinkers and who can negotiate the rapids if necessary. As one foxy CEO said: "It's the bombshell you don't expect that can do you in. The best protection is to have commanders under you who can make split-second decisions under enemy fire. Each decision may not be for the best, but the next one corrects what's bad about the previous one. So the chain of decisions holds up in the end." Clearly, this has not been the case with the way mad cow disease has been handled in Europe. Ministers have had to resign because at first they didn't take the issue seriously enough and responded with denials that there was a problem. Now the pendulum has swung the other way, and governments are trying to make up lost ground with draconian laws which could jeopardise the beef industry. As if that is not enough, European farmers' misery has been compounded by the outbreak of foot-and-mouth disease. The latter is so contagious that strong measures are a necessity to halt it. All in all, a cool, foxy head is required to steer any country affected through these shoals of uncertainty.

Sam Walton, the founder of Wal-Mart Stores, which is now the largest retailer in the world with over one million employees, was a fox. He spent most of his time away from his office visiting the stores, checking standards and more importantly inspiring his staff to think of ways of doing things differently and better. He walked the walk. He had a good nose for business and was forever sniffing out promising innovations developed at store level which could be applied throughout the group. This is in marked contrast to hedgehog leaders who hibernate in their penthouse suites surrounded by their equally aloof, hedgehog-like assistants. They seldom venture out of the cloistered calm of their offices to meet real people in the real world – but then they feel it is unnecessary to do so since they've already worked out the grand solution. To all intents and purposes, hedgehog leaders are invisible except for the odd photograph and ceremonial function. They rule by remote control.

Have you seen the movie *Brassed Off*? It's about a brass band from a Yorkshire colliery winning the national championships against the background of the closure of the colliery. In one scene, a young female executive asks the managing director whether he has read her viability study into ways of keeping the pit open. He says no, the decision to close was taken two years ago and coal is history. Her retort is that clearly reports have to be seen to be written rather than written to be seen. That's the way sleek head-office hedgehogs like it!

The unnatural, inward-looking and incestuous atmosphere of a hedgehog lair resembles that of a royal court of old plagued by intrigue and infighting among the courtiers. The only measure of success is how favourable a courtier's standing is with the king or queen. In the resulting competition in which each courtier is vying for the eye of the monarch, the hedgehog species show their expertise at stabbing their rivals in the back. They have so many spikes to do it with! Conspiracy theories abound, and any questioning of the party line laid down by the ruler is viewed as treachery. Niccolò Machiavelli, the sixteenth-century Florentine philosopher who promoted the use of unscrupulous statecraft to preserve power, would have been quite at home in the company of modern, smooth-talking hedgehogs. The only thing he would find unfamiliar in today's world is the speed of travel and communication which has reduced us to a global village. Unfortunately, it has also produced a superclass of globe-trotting hedgehogs with no fixed abode and no fixed commitments to any community or country. Their entire time is spent chasing the bucks across national boundaries, cooped up in the intensive care of a 747's first-class cabin. You can be sure that if Machiavelli had been alive at the beginning of the 21st century, he would have had multiple passports, several aliases and would be clocking up millions of air miles. Even as the prince of hedgehogs, he had respect for the fox. He had this to say about his rival: "As a prince must be able to act just like a beast, he should learn from the fox and the lion; because the lion does not defend himself against traps, and the fox does not defend himself against wolves. So one has to be a fox in order to recognise traps, and a lion to frighten off wolves."

It goes without saying that hedgehogs are natural centralisers who want to achieve change from the top down. They are conceited enough to think they have all the answers for the working classes. Development – with a capital "D" – should radiate out from the centre. Foxy executives, on the other hand, support the idea of change from the bottom up. Decentralisation, without losing all control, is the name of the game for the business fox. On a slightly different note but in the same context, foxy monarchs in the old days used to employ court jesters with the aim of the latter bending the royal ear with unorthodox opinions on matters of state. As they say, there's many a truth that lies in jest. Nevertheless, the court jester had to invest considerable humour in putting across his contrarian views in order to make the sovereign laugh and thus minimise his chances of being beheaded! We naturally choose friends that we agree with, but we learn something new from people with whom we don't. An old Spanish adage goes as follows: "He who advises is not the traitor." So, in plain English, don't shoot the messenger.

A lesson from Mother Nature, flying frogs and sea-foxes

You needn't have salt water coursing through your veins to imagine the following analogy: an angling hedgehog, if there ever was one, would prefer to fish within the known, protective waters of a cove where the effects of tide and winds are relatively certain and controllable. In contrast, a sea-fox would prefer to investigate other fishing grounds beyond the protective waters of the cove and be willing to operate in the uncertain and uncontrollable elements of the open sea.

Thus, an essential element in the difference between the mind-set of the fox and the hedgehog is the fox's preparedness to strike out for the unknown. This in turn means an acceptance that mistakes do happen. What is more, mistakes are not just golden opportunities for learning; they are, in fact, sometimes the *only* opportunity for learning something truly new and making progress. In 1928, Alexander Fleming discovered penicillin accidentally when he saw that a bit of mould, which had fallen from a culture plate in his laboratory, had destroyed bacteria around it. Basically, he won the Nobel Prize, and a knighthood into the bargain, for a mistake which he had the intelligence to follow up on.

Hedgehogs balk at this approach because it may well expose them to peer ridicule. Indeed, they view mistakes in two possible lights. If it is somebody else's, that person is to blame because somebody has to be held responsible and punished. If the mistake is their own, no-one is to blame because it was the result of circumstances beyond anyone's control. In the latter case, hedgehogs are very good at producing an expression of injured innocence, reminding one of professional footballers about to be given a yellow or red card for a foul. Either way, mistakes are perceived by hedgehogs as aberrations which don't advance you up the learning curve. Failure has the same penalty attached to it as drawing the "chance" or "community chest" card in a game of Monopoly that says: do not pass go, do not collect £200, move directly to jail! Better be right all the time is the maxim of the cautious hedgehog; or at least don't be caught out if you're wrong.

Foxes can take solace from the fact that their approach to learning and problem-solving has been used successfully for many years by the world's most powerful and foxy CEO – Mother Nature. As pointed out by Professor Daniel C. Dennet, the Director of Cognitive Studies at Tufts University in Medford, Massachusetts: "For evolution, which knows nothing, the leaps into novelty are blindly taken by mutations, which are copying 'errors' in the DNA. Most of these are fatal errors, in fact. Since the vast majority of mutations are harmful, the process of natural selection actually works to keep the mutation rate very low. Fortunately for us, it *does not achieve perfect success*, for if it did, evolution would finally grind to a halt, its sources of novelty dried up."

This is particularly evident in the enigmatic rain forests of Borneo which boast one of the largest concentrations of gliders – at least thirty different species of animals as diverse as lizards, squirrels, lemurs or colugos, snakes, geckos and frogs – that have changed their physiological structure over the years to allow them to glide from tree to tree. Why is this island so rich in gliding species while other rain forests like the Amazon have none? The answer – Mother Nature and evolution. The rain forests of South East Asia are dominated by giant dipterocarp trees which tend to crowd out other trees and, to add insult to injury, offer hungry residents infrequent and unpredictable bounties of fruit. To work within this context of inconsistent and non-controllable food sources, the frogs and other animals that lived within the area took to an ingenious way of moving from one arboreal restaurant to another – jumping large distances. A creative strategy indeed! They realised that this provided the most effective way of getting around without excessive climbing and exposure to the danger of predators. Gradually they evolved to a more manageable mode of movement – *gliding*. Understandably this didn't happen overnight, nor without its fair share of bruised and battered little bodies. But it was all part of the learning experience.

The point of the gliding, flying frogs? The mind-set of making mistakes and learning from them to expand one's knowledge, so intrinsic to the mind of the fox, is nothing new. It is a natural process, and it has been around for millions of years. The other important lesson to derive from this example is: *think the unthinkable*. A frog that glides? You're pulling my leg. But it's a fact like the flying hedgehogs in the previous section – except that the latter travel first class! Mind you, in the world of political affairs, the Florida recount in the US presidential election was also unthinkable until it happened in 2000.

How else can the advance in the forest gliders be construed to be of relevance to the global economy? How can those blessed with a higher cognitive function than a flying lizard benefit from this insight? Humans have the tendency to try and pre-empt a future to which they link adverse consequences by taking actions to head it off. To a risk-averse person there is nothing wrong with this strategy. Ironically, however, such restrictive thinking was not the type that laid the foundations for, and made possible, a global economy. The great explorers of the past, like Marco Polo, David Livingstone and Christopher Columbus were all foxes who were responsible for establishing trade routes and the exchange of ideas and cultures. The hedgehogs followed in their tracks as settlers. Much of the time these pioneering foxes didn't know where they were going. Columbus thought he was heading for Asia, but intercepted America by chance.

Indeed, in determining their position at sea, the early navigators implemented a learn-from-mistakes philosophy. They would first make a guess about where they were. Next, they estimated – to the nearest nautical mile – their latitude and longitude. After that, they worked out how high in the sky the sun would reach at midday if, by some incredible coincidence, that *was* their actual position. They would then measure the actual elevation of the sun, compare the figures and adjust their initial estimate accordingly. If they were still wrong, they would indulge in a process of iteration till they obtained an answer that was approximately correct. Today, on the same principle of taking the plunge and then revising one's position in light of further information, the global economy is being significantly reshaped by the new-age sea-foxes – the Internet pioneers. Take Amazon.com and eBay. The former, even with its ups and downs, has revolutionised retailing with its on-line marketing of books. The other set up a website which has changed the nature of auctioneering forever. Have you ever heard of cyber-fleas? Probably not, but eBay is the world's biggest cyber-fleamarket. You can sell or buy almost anything on the site. At the heart of eBay's success is that nobody in the world of bricks and mortar can imitate it. Its uniqueness lies in its virtuality.

A philosophical interlude
and moment for introspection

Pause here for a second and ponder: "OK, what am I? A hedgehog or a fox?" Whether we like it or not, most senior business people are more likely to be of the prickly variety. Hedgehogs, according to Isaiah Berlin in his celebrated essay *The Hedgehog and the Fox*, "relate everything to a central vision, one system less or more coherent or articulate, in terms of which they understand, think and feel". The twentieth-century accent on strategic planning with rigid structures and objectives has made employees march unquestioningly to the same tune. But managerial hedgehogs shouldn't worry; they share the same characteristics as writers and philosophers of the likes of Dante, Plato, Hegel, Dostoevsky, Nietzsche and Proust. You may ask why there is such a preponderance of hedgehogs in the senior ranks of business today. Well, most senior managers are middle-aged folk who belong to a generation where lifetime employment was *the idea*. Back in the last century, parents would send their children to respectable schools so that they could qualify to go to respectable universities and thereafter join respectable organisations – for life. From womb to tomb, twentieth-century man was programmed to be a hedgehog. The fact that this world is vanishing fast is leading to a much higher proportion of the younger generation becoming foxes. The 21st century belongs to them.

Nevertheless, what cannot be denied is that, over the last few hundred years, business has owed a great deal to the foxes. These, according to Berlin, "pursue many ends, often unrelated and even contradictory. Their thought is often scattered or diffused, moving on many levels, seizing upon the vast variety of experiences." In the world of philosophy and literature, full foxy points go to the likes of Shakespeare, Aristotle, Molière and Goethe but, in the commercial sphere, we must not overlook foxy families like the Medicis, the Rothschilds and the Rockefellers.

Bertrand Russell, a fox of considerable stature in British philosophy in the last century, gave a delightful description of how differently hedgehog and foxy philosophers arrive at the truth. Hedgehogs, like the German philosopher Gottfried Leibniz, produce a vast edifice of deduction pyramided upon a pinpoint of logical principle. Foxes draw comparatively modest conclusions from a broad survey of many facts. If a principle proposed by a hedgehog "is completely true and the deductions are entirely valid, all is well; but the structure is unstable, and the slightest flaw anywhere brings it down in ruins". As against this, a philosophical fox such as John Locke or David Hume makes sure that the base of the pyramid "is on the solid ground of observed fact, and the pyramid tapers upward, not downward; consequently the equilibrium is stable, and a flaw here or there can be rectified without total disaster".

Interestingly, Immanuel Kant, the greatest philosopher in modern times who died at the ripe old age of eighty in 1804, was a hybridised version of the two creatures we are talking about – in other words he was a "hedgefox". In his masterly book, *The Critique of Pure Reason*, he combined the pronouncements of the rational and empirical schools of philosophy. The former states that, through pure reasoning, you can derive the meaning of existence and everything else in the world from first principles (hedgehog stuff). The other maintains that the only source of knowledge is experience (foxy stuff). Kant drew on both perspectives to come up with his theory of synthetic *a priori* propositions like "every event has a cause". He argued that this belief could not be divorced from experience but neither could it be derived from experience. It was part of our inherent nature to believe that every cause has an effect (and vice versa) in that it gives coherence to our perceptions. Hence, the concept of cause and effect transcended experience.

The greatest mind of the twentieth century, Albert Einstein, was also a hedgefox. Like Plato, he believed that you could shed light on the mysteries of the universe by sitting in an armchair and contemplating the problem in a single-minded manner. You could even play thought experiments in your mind and see where they led. However, unlike Plato and like a true fox, he believed that all theories had to be grounded in fact and confirmed by observation. For example, in 1905 he presented his special theory of relativity, which included the famous equation $E = mc^2$. It was only in 1945 with the detonation of the atom bomb that the equation was verified. Likewise, in 1916, when he introduced the general theory of relativity, it contained the entirely new concepts of space being curved and light rays being bent in a gravitational field. These were subsequently confirmed in 1919 by observations of how starlight curved around an eclipsed sun. In brief, his two famous quotes sum up his philosophy of life: "God may be sophisticated, but He is not malicious" and "God does not play dice". As he grew older, his hedgehog side came to the fore with his attempt to develop a unified field theory which explained everything. Then, when he failed, he tried to prove it was impossible. And when he failed to do that either, he worried that no-one else would ever lay the matter to rest!

Einstein's example implies that, if you are going to be a hedgefox, the prime time to be one is between the ages of 25 and 40. On the one hand, you still retain the arrogance of youth to challenge mainstream orthodoxies; on the other hand, you have experienced something of the world at large to see how diverse it is. Einstein was 26 when he announced the special theory of relativity and 37 when he launched the general theory. It is no coincidence that most of the great advances in physics and mathematics were achieved by relatively young geniuses. The Nobel Prize comes much later on, once the idea has become generally accepted. It must be hard to live with yourself if you were so much cleverer when you were young!

Moving to the East, foxes make use of the Chinese philosophy of Yin and Yang in that they understand the need for balance between the many opposing elements we face in this world. We live in a state of permanent contradiction, wondering whether to be just or merciful; tough or gentle; bold or cautious; competitive or co-operative. Indeed, we're perfectly happy to carry completely conflicting beliefs in our mind, skipping from one to the other. For instance, when tragedy strikes, we believe in predestination – what will be, will be. At other times, we believe that life is about what we decide to do of our own free will. Is the universe infinite in time and space, or did it start with a big bang and its boundaries are now expanding? One or other view must be right, but they can't both be right at the same time. Kant called these paradoxes "antinomies". He used them to justify his rejection of pure rationalism on the one hand and pure empiricism on the other. For a more homely antinomy, consider the wisdom contained in these two old saws: "birds of a feather flock together" and "opposites attract". We accept both of them! And then there is the antinomy which lies at the heart of capitalism. Individual companies want to crush the competition in order to maximise their own profits. Yet competition is good for society as a whole.

Foxy judges and juries in particular have to keep opposites in mind as they listen to the persuasive arguments of the prosecution and defence. It is only when they've heard all sides of the case that they make a judgement of "guilty" or "not guilty". Two-party democracies like the American one are supposed to offer alternative versions of the political truth to electors. Lately, the Republicans and Democrats have been awfully alike in their policies. It is only when you have disputes like the Florida recount that the knives really come out with the lawyers in tow. A foxy CEO of Coca-Cola Enterprises had this to say at a university commencement address several years ago: "Imagine life as a game in which you are juggling five balls in the air. You name them – work, family, health, friends and spirit – and you're keeping all of these in the air. You will soon understand that work is a rubber ball. If you drop it, it will bounce back. But the other four balls – family, health, friends and spirit – are made of glass. If you drop one of these, they will be irrevocably scuffed, marked, nicked or even shattered. They will never be the same. You must understand that and strive for balance in your life." But here's the rub: success in work usually comes with single-mindedness. Another contradiction! As *Business Week* said in a recent issue: "The fundamental task of today's CEO is simplicity itself: get the stock price up. Period."

In contrast to foxes, hedgehogs view the world through ideologically tinted spectacles which let in no other light besides that which is on the same wavelength as their idea. They're excellent at selective reporting of the facts. Moreover, because they focus on their idea in isolation, they ignore the critical interdependencies that make up complete systems. Hence, they will often press so hard for an idea that they mess up the workings of the system as a whole. They don't see the trade-offs, and so they run into the law of unintended consequences where the world is worse off than if they had not intervened at all. This happens particularly with hedgehog-like development agencies who impose their own solutions on local communities rather than finding out what they want in the first place. Ignorance of

cultural differences is often at the heart of costly development mistakes. A classic case of the aforementioned law in
action was the establishment of irrigation schemes in the
Sudan which immediately led to an increase in diseases associated with water-borne bugs. The way the colonial powers drew the boundaries in Africa is hard to beat. On a different front, everybody said that casinos in South Africa
would create jobs. They've had precisely the opposite effect. Wherever they've been erected, they've drained the local economy of money as poor people – seduced by the
dream of becoming instant millionaires – have frittered
away their hard-earned, meagre incomes on the slot ma-
chines. Consequently, local businesses and shops have suf-
fered and have had to lay off staff.

Nowhere can a hedgehog's blinkered approach better be
illustrated than in the environmental field. We all know that
we cannot allow the environment to be destroyed – it must
be preserved for future generations. Equally, we know that
economic development is crucial for the improvement in
life of the masses of poor people on this Earth. So, somewhere there has to be a compromise, as the phrase "sustainable development" implies. Neither deeply green hedgehogs who only press the environmental button nor dark
blue hedgehogs only interested in economic growth have
the answer. In fact, the best definition of sustainable development comes from a Norwegian fox, Gro Harlem Brundtland, who popularised the phrase in the first place. Not
only was she Prime Minister of Norway, she also chaired
the World Commission on Environment and Development
which published the Brundtland Report in 1987 entitled
Our Common Future. In it, sustainable development was defined as: "Development which meets the needs of the present generation without compromising the ability for future
generations to meet their needs." Beguilingly simple, but it

says it all. Subsequently, more detailed definitions have been published, but they do not come close to this single pearl of wisdom. However, when all is said and done in the environmental debate, foxes acknowledge that extremists can advance the boundaries of knowledge through the Hegelian approach of thesis and antithesis leading to synthesis. Somebody has to push the edge of the envelope on either side to set new standards for the middle ground.

Tiger Woods, for a different reason, can also be nominated as a philosophical fox. He is a student of what the Japanese call *Kaizen* – a striving for continual improvement to the extreme point of testing something until it breaks and then analysing *why* it broke. The results are thereafter assimilated into future designs and applications. In a similar way and like the navigators of old, the scientific method demands that a scientist, after establishing a hypothesis, continually tests it to *disprove* or reject it. If the hypothesis survives the trauma of testing, it is embraced as probable fact. As Sir Arthur Conan Doyle's famous detective, Sherlock Holmes, once remarked to his faithful assistant Dr Watson: "How often have I said to you, that when you have eliminated the impossible, whatever remains, however improbable, must be the truth?" What he was possibly suggesting is that eliminating what one can't do provides a more revealing insight into what is possible. By approaching the cognitive process in the Sherlock Holmes way, we will not only be more accurately informed but also make more effective decisions. Often the best way of choosing your favourite person or thing is to start at the bottom and reject your obvious dislikes. Then you gradually work upwards until you're comparing your top two preferences to make your final decision.

Cluedo, the popular detective game, illustrates Holmes's point perfectly. The way to win the game and identify the murderer of the owner of Tudor Close is to eliminate all the other suspects. If Colonel Mustard didn't do it with the candlestick in the conservatory, then it might have been Miss Scarlett with the dagger in the study – and so on. Another example is this well-known riddle: if you come to a crossroads and meet two locals, one of whom always tells the truth and the other one always tells lies, and you don't know which is which, what question do you ask to ensure that you get to St Ives? The answer is: "What would the other fellow say if I asked him?" Whichever person you asked, you would know that the answer is false, discard it and take the opposite route. As Holmes would say: "It's elementary, my dear Watson." In the quiz show *Who Wants To Be A Millionaire?* it is as important to be adept at eliminating wrong answers as it is to have a feel for the right one, especially when you're close to the million!

Foxy parents get their young children to do something by telling them *not* to do it. In a similar vein, Nelson Mandela once gave a very foxy definition of leadership: "A leader is like a shepherd. He stays behind the flock, letting the most nimble go on ahead, whereupon the others follow, not realising that all along they are being directed from behind." So once again, are you a hedgehog or a fox? Or maybe a bit of both? If you're the last, you're lucky to be so special. In the business world, hedgefoxes play the crucial role of bridging the gap between hedgehogs to whom they easily relate and foxes for whom they act as corporate crusaders.

Tiger and the *Titanic* provide clues

As Tiger, the fox of the fairway, navigates the hallowed greens of the world's greatest golf courses, the philosophy of *Kaizen* has equipped him to optimise on every bit of fortune and misfortune that comes his way. He is an obsessive student of both the game and his play. He continually reviews video footage of old tournaments – even those he has won – to criticise his play and to look for any information, no matter how trivial or apparently contradictory, that will allow him to make more accurate decisions when playing any course, under any conditions and against any other player.

The result: as he prepares for a tournament, he has a firm understanding of what lies inside and outside his control. For a start, he has a thorough knowledge of the rules of the game of golf and any recent revisions governing not only play but also the range of equipment that can be used. Obviously, he knows that he has no control whatsoever over the content of the rulebook: it controls him. No individual golfer, however awesome, has the power to change the rules. He can submit a proposal for a change if he thinks a particular rule is ridiculous; but until the relevant governing body in golf has considered it, he must abide by what's laid down in the book. So what Tiger does control is his knowledge of the rules: what he doesn't control is the content of the rules themselves.

The same applies to the layout of the course. Tiger can't change that. But he can play practice rounds to get a feel for each hole; and he and his caddie can measure the yardages and decide on the optimum strategy to be adopted for each hole. Again, he has no control over the strengths and the weaknesses and the overall capabilities of the other players. However, he can make himself familiar with their style of play; and he knows that, on the last day of the tournament, if he is breathing down their necks going into the final stretch, many of them will wilt under pressure! The weather: that's an important element during a tournament that is outside everybody's control. Tiger may have a general idea of the kind of conditions that will probably prevail; but he certainly won't know until the actual day, and sometimes only at the time of his actual shot, whether the wind is blowing or not and in what direction; whether it's sunny or raining; and what the temperature is.

Broadly, in the lead-up to the tournament, he classifies everything into those things he can control: his swing, his selection of clubs, his state of mind, his knowledge of the course; and those things that he cannot control: the rules of the tournament, the layout of the course, the quality of the other players, the weather conditions. Equally, he divides all factors into those of which he is certain and those of which he is uncertain. Of the things he doesn't control, he can be certain of the rules and the layout of the course; but he can't be certain about the weather and the level at which the other players will perform on the actual day. Of the things over which he has control, he can be certain of the number of clubs that he will have in his bag; but he won't know the actual club that he will choose for a shot until he has examined all the options before he plays the shot. More importantly, he doesn't know in advance what score he is going to shoot because there's many a slip between cup and lip. The decision he takes for each shot after weighing up the various scenarios may or may not have the desired outcome. There are no guarantees, even for Tiger Woods. He is sometimes in the rough and sometimes even out of bounds.

Hopefully, this exposition on Tiger's cognitive processes is giving you a clue as to where our thoughts are leading us when we explore the mind of the fox. But, like the good foxes we are, in order to make the trail even clearer, we want to provide a negative example – something which exhibits all the worst traits of hedgehogs. We can think of nothing better than the events which led up to the sinking of the *Titanic* at 2:20 am on 15 April 1912. It was the ship's maiden voyage; and the disaster, which occurred at the zenith of Britain's imperial authority on the world stage, was never entertained as a scenario by the company that owned the ship, the engineers who constructed it or the captain who sailed it. The ship was deemed unsinkable. After all, it had a double-bottomed hull that was divided into sixteen watertight compartments; and for the ship to sink, more than four of these compartments had to be flooded. It followed from this overambitious reasoning that the *Titanic* was not equipped with a sufficient number of lifeboats, and the crew did not properly conduct lifeboat drills for the passengers at the beginning of the voyage. Moreover, at the time of the disaster, the ship was steaming too fast in view of the fact that the bridge had been warned of icebergs in the vicinity. The consequence: five of the *Titanic*'s compartments were ripped open in a glancing blow with an iceberg; 1 513 souls went to a watery grave; and a terrible price was paid for the conceit of the imperial hedgehogs who literally believed that Britannia ruled the waves.

In retrospect, the participants in the *Titanic* project should have done an analysis of what they could and could not control. No way could they control the state of the ocean; yet they definitely controlled the safety features of the ship. Secondly, while they could be certain about the performance parameters of the liner under normal conditions, they couldn't be certain about all the possible conditions which the ship might meet on its voyages. Hence, all those eminent minds fell into the trap of ignoring the unthinkable – and that's how accidents happen. Today, a growing number of companies are hiring risk management experts, with the specific objective of painting "unthinkable" scenarios for the SHE (safety, health and the environment) aspects of their business. Four key questions are normally asked. What are the types of accidents that can happen? What is their probability of occurrence? What will the severity of the impact be if they do? And what are we reasonably going to do to minimise or eliminate the risk of those accidents? In light of tougher SHE legislation being introduced everywhere in the world to hold companies and individuals accountable for their actions, answers to these questions are as important as the examination of the risks of fraud, corruption and theft in the financial area, which is usually done by internal audit departments. The silly thing is that there is no trade-off between good SHE practice and the bottom line. When workers believe management care, they work harder.

Our foxy matrix

This brings us to the essential purpose of this book which is to analyse how a fox thinks and acts. If, after the brief bout of introspection we recommended you undertake earlier on, you decided you were a 24-carat hedgehog, the material that follows attempts to persuade you to become a fox. If, however, all things considered, the mirror responded that you were already a fox, don't stop reading – chances are that we can improve your mental processes so that you become an even more effective fox.

You may well ask: can you ever turn a hedgehog into a fox? The answer is: retrench him and see! But, seriously, in this day and age of more and more people having to work for themselves, necessity is the mother of invention and even the most stolid hedgehogs have to change. And it's never too late, as the large preponderance of silver foxes who would otherwise have been retired can testify. The more interesting question is whether any foxes become hedgehogs. The answer is plenty, for – as you will see – it's much harder staying at the top than getting there in the first place. Entrepreneurs who are foxy whilst they are building up their businesses turn into the most reprehensible hedge-hogs once they've accumulated the money, the power and the prestige. The trouble comes when a fox starts believing too much in his own judgement and in his own press. Hunger is replaced by laziness. Overconfidence ousts self-questioning and self-criticism. Success breeds complacency and complacency breeds hedgehogs. Thus, the humble fox who took nothing for granted in the beginning becomes an arrogant hedgehog in the end who has delusions of grandeur and knows he's right. And we all know pride comes before the fall. That's why so few businesses last fifty years. Those that start out as losers go bankrupt first; and the majority of those that start out as winners are subsequently killed by their success. Besides being sophisticated, God is also a Great Equaliser!

Long-term success in the commercial sphere is therefore a rarity. You can see the truth of this statement also in the field of sport and the arts, where you can count the truly great in any category on one hand. They are individuals who don't just make it to the summit – they stay there for a long time because they never lose the edge. Examples are Pele in football; Gareth Edwards in rugby; Donald Bradman in cricket; Mohammed Ali in boxing; Carl Lewis in athletics; Pete Sampras and Martina Navratilova in tennis; Jack Nicklaus in golf; Margot Fonteyn and Rudolf Nureyev in ballet; Charles Dickens in literature; John Gielgud in films and Picasso in art. Then there were The Beatles: they not only dominated the 1960s but are still No. 1, which happens to be the title of their latest album of original hits. Being a champion does not exclude going through a bad patch. But you bounce back – like André Agassi and comeback kid Jennifer Capriati who both won the 2001 Australian Open tennis championship. Will Tiger Woods join this star-studded cast of foxes? Only time will tell.

Before introducing our foxy matrix, a word of caution. We do not want this book to be lumped in the same category as all those heavy management treatises incorporating matrices which offer the ultimate solution for the readers' happiness. Our matrix is neither the be-all and end-all of business, nor is it a shatteringly brilliant new concept to take your breath away. Rather, as we will demonstrate, it sets out in a simple fashion how human beings naturally think in their pristine, foxy state – before they've been conned into accepting some artificially rigid thinking device marketed as the new way to plan strategically ahead.

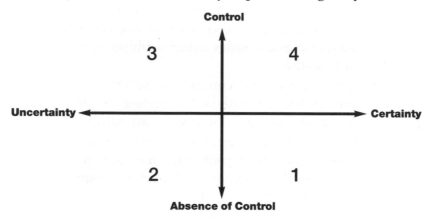

Our matrix has two axes: the horizontal one portrays certainty and uncertainty and the vertical one control and the absence of control. These two axes yield four quadrants: the bottom right-hand one represents things that are certain but outside our control. Then going clockwise, the bottom left-hand one encompasses things that are both uncertain and outside our control; the top left-hand one things which are uncertain but within our control; and the top right-hand one things which are certain and within our control.

Quite a large number of people never stray from a particular quadrant. Those who restrict themselves to the first quadrant tend to be *fatalists* who know what's going to happen, but feel they cannot do anything about it. People keeping to the second quadrant are *dice-rollers* who believe that everything in life happens purely by chance. The third quadrant is inhabited by *fence-sitters* who feel a certain sense of control, but are eternally ambivalent. They meet themselves coming the other way in arguments. The fourth and last quadrant is occupied by the *control freaks* who know exactly what is going to happen because they believe that they are totally in control. This is where most of the hedgehogs sit.

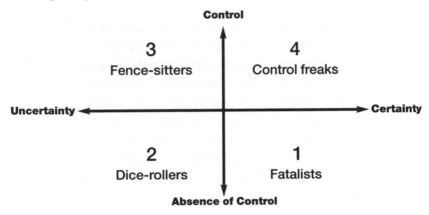

Foxes are none of these species but borrow from all of them. You can't box a fox! Hence, the matrix has to be modified to the one shown on the next page.

The most important aspect of the newly constituted matrix follows Sherlock Holmes's line of thinking: first eliminate the impossible before concentrating on the possible. To put it slightly differently, if you want to be truly in charge of your destiny, you first require to know your limitations and be humbler than you think. Hence, the lower layer of the matrix which many people ignore lays a solid foundation for effective thinking in the upper part.

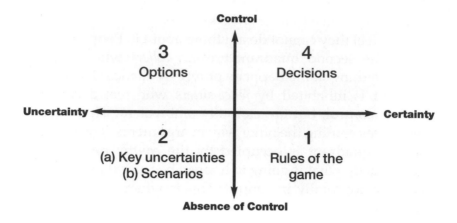

The first quadrant now represents the rules of the game – things that are certain and over which we have no control. The second quadrant has two components: key uncertainties over which we also have no control; and plausible and relevant scenarios derived from these uncertainties, though the scenarios must be vivid and different enough to take us out of the comfort zone. The third quadrant is now identified with the options presented by the scenarios. The formulation of options is crucial and allows us to operate with more control in an uncertain environment. The fourth quadrant is the area where decisions are made based on the preferred scenario and linked to the preferred option. It is also the quadrant where strategic plans and programmes of action should be located, as these are really decision paths formulated in advance. The term "scenario planning" normally denotes the processes one goes through in the first two quadrants. "Rules of the game" are sometimes called "predetermined elements" and "key uncertainties" are "driving forces". Otherwise, nothing is different in terms of the methodology.

Instead of the more restrictive, cognitive model used by hedgehogs that operates solely on the right-hand side of the matrix, this model goes beyond such linear thinking. Handling uncertainty in a systematic and realistic manner provides a real competitive advantage to companies that want to be imaginative; it paves the way for a strategic conversation about the future without reams of paperwork and computer runs being required in advance; it serves up strategic insights without getting mired down in too much detail and it is comprehensive without being pretentious.

Our matrix, in essence, represents the mind of the fox. The model also partially answers the question why scenario planning has failed to catch on in the corporate world in the same way that strategic planning has. CEOs abhor uncertainty. They can't stand ambiguity and ambivalence. Their attitude is encapsulated in that famous phrase "give me a one-armed economist that doesn't say 'on the one hand and on the other'". However, the fault also lies with the scenario planners themselves who sometimes come across as intellectuals in an ivory tower, using precious language which is out of touch with the shop floor.

The model may sound complicated with plenty of bells and whistles: but it's not. In practice, we work through the matrix and draw scenarios every day of our lives. Imagine the following situation: you are driving down a main road and there is a crossroads ahead. You are on the main road, and logic and law dictate that you have the right of way. This can be referred to as the *rule of the game*. However, on the minor road travelling at right angles to you and towards the intersection is another vehicle that, theoretically, should stop. This action is out of your control, cannot be guaranteed and is, therefore, uncertain. This is a *key uncertainty*. In your mind you play out different *scenarios*:

1. The driver of the other car sees you and slows to a halt, allowing you to travel through safely.

2. The driver of the other car doesn't see you, drives

straight through the intersection, and you have a near miss.

3. The driver of the other car doesn't see you, drives straight through the intersection and you crash.

Based on the scenarios, you have a number of *options*:

1. Maintain your speed on the assumption that the driver is eventually going to see you.

2. Slow down because you worry that the driver is not going to see you.

3. Speed up in the hope that you may get through the intersection before the other car arrives.

Options 1 and 3 may result in a crash, whereas option 2 won't. These options will influence your *decision*. In a matter of seconds, you have just worked through the matrix. If you have a cautious temperament, you'll choose option 2. If you don't, you'll go for 1 or 3.

Another situation we have all been in when we were young, and when the matrix is definitely used, is the telephone call asking someone out on a first date. The rules of the game are simple: you have no chance at all if you don't talk to your intended date; if you come on too strong, you may put him/her off; but if you act too casual, you may not get the message across. The key uncertainty is simple: you don't know how the person on the other end of the phone is going to react to anything you say. The scenarios are infinite because the conversation can go in any direction. The options are to take the leap and ask up front; or start cautiously, see how the land lies and possibly pop the question of a date later on. And then you decide, intellectually or impulsively, what to do. It brings to mind rose-petal scenarios of the type "she loves me, she loves me not" as a young lover pulls each petal off the flower!

Further down the line, the matrix is an excellent way of judging whether you want to enter into matrimony with the lady or gentleman in question. The rules of the game can be summed up in the wedding vow you make to your partner "to have and to hold from this day forward, for better for worse, for richer for poorer, in sickness and in health, to love and to cherish, till death do us part". The key uncertainty is whether you do indeed continue to love each other or grow estranged. In the first case, you don't have to consider options for you *will* stay together. In the second case, the options are clear: stick together and make the marriage work or part company with possible repercussions on the kids if any. Couples in the second category have to decide for themselves which course of action is right. And they often reverse their decisions.

Memories of the future

Because scenarios are stories that unfold in a sequentially organised manner, they can be viewed as multiple pathways into the future. Each path denotes a hypothetical condition of the environment to which an option for action can be attached: if the future turns out this way, I will do that. According to David Ingvar, the head of the Neurobiology Department at the University of Lund in Sweden, these paths are stored in the prefrontal lobes of our brain. The more we walk down them in our minds, the more we remember them. In other words, we are continually forming a "memory of the future" in our imagination and revisiting it time and again.

In his research, David Ingvar addresses the question as to what function this "memory of the future" might serve and why it would have evolved. Apart from giving us a filter to help us deal with the mass of information that we encounter, it prepares us for action once one of the visited futures materialises. In other words, it gives us the best possible leverage in advance to deal with a wide range of future developments and outcomes. A good example of where this theory is applied in practice is the use of simulators to train pilots to fly aircraft. By the time they pass the final exam, it must be second nature to them what to do in all situations but especially emergency ones. In the latter case, they won't have time to scroll through an instruction manual like the one they have for landing. The rules of the game for flying, the key uncertainties during flight, the range of scenarios that you may have to face as a pilot, the options open to you to respond and the selection of the correct option must be ingrained. It's a pity that CEOs don't go through simulator training before they fly their businesses into the future. Of the largest 100 companies in the world in the 1950s, 70 have disappeared without a trace. Imagine taking a flight where there was only a 30 per cent probability of landing safely!

Few things are certain in this life, but especially in business. In many ways uncertainty, the natural field of operations of the fox, offers a real challenge for business, but it also opens up the doors for development. It is sad, therefore, that big business today is a century behind the physicists who in 1900 embraced uncertainty in that most "certain" branch of science – physics. The study of elementary particles has given rise to the exciting field of quantum physics that takes the deterministic picture of the universe offered by Isaac Newton and blows it wide open. According to Paul Davies, a theoretical physicist and Professor of Natural Philosophy at the University of Adelaide in Australia, even the common-sense rule of cause and effect that we referred to earlier is suspended at the atomic level. The rule of law is replaced by a sort of anarchy or chaos where things happen spontaneously and without certainty. Particles of matter may simply pop into existence without warning, and then equally abruptly disappear again. Or a particle in one place may suddenly materialise in another place, or reverse its direction of motion. If you think this is odd, please answer the question: do you believe in miracles? If you do, then you also believe that things occasionally happen for no earthly reason.

In contrast, modern-day business is positively Newtonian in its outlook and trails behind science in its rate of development. Business still takes a deterministic view of the world. It pictures it running like clockwork. As long as one can analyse the inner workings of the clock in minute detail, one can predict exactly what the mechanism is going to do in the foreseeable future. Actually, there is so much competition, so much discontinuity in the markets and so many new horizons that are opening up as a result of technological change that the only thing that is certain is uncertainty. Businesses therefore have to work within this uncertainty and require a complexity-reduction process to do so. In this respect, our foxy matrix offers an ideal way to gather all the relevant information, sift it like sand running through an hourglass and use it to focus on the most realistic options available at any one time. The final decision is more informed; but if it proves to be wrong, the decision maker can return to the matrix for another round.

SWOT – a nuts and bolts explanation

Readers may well ask where SWOT analysis (strengths, weaknesses, opportunities and threats) fits into our matrix. The answer is that the matrix now changes the sequence to OTSW: opportunities and threats are outside our control whereas we can do something about our strengths and weaknesses. Opportunities and threats therefore belong to the first two quadrants on the lower deck, and strengths and weaknesses to the last two quadrants on the upper deck.

Let us consider the example of a proud owner of a hardware store in a small country town. We'll call him John. The opportunity may well be that the only other hardware store in town is about to close because the owner has made it known that he is going to retire. If John is certain about this information, it is a rule of the game. If it is a rumour it is a key uncertainty. Either way, it offers John an opportunity to expand his business. The converse is that John has heard that a big supermarket chain is intending to establish a new branch in the town. It will have a hardware section which will offer considerable discounts and a variety of goods to customers. That is a threat. Again, depending on the credibility of the source of this news, its appropriate place is in the first or the second quadrant of the matrix.

John now considers his strengths and weaknesses and his options in light of them. One of his strengths is customer loyalty because his shop has been around a long time and he likes to chat to his customers; and they like to chat to him. His option in the "opportunity" scenario just outlined is to persuade these customers to speak to those who have frequented the other shop and tell them what a decent deal they can get at his shop. Word of mouth may suffice. Another option may be to drop leaflets in their letter boxes. John also realises that one of his weaknesses is that he doesn't carry some of the brand names that the other shop does. His option is to expand his range of hardware and correct this situation or stick to his traditional lines and try and convince his new customers to switch brands.

In the "threat" scenario of a retail giant arriving in town, John may opt to build on his strong customer loyalty by making his shop even more welcoming – by putting say a little coffee stall inside. If he pursues this strategy, he will be going out of his way to differentiate himself from the impersonal surroundings of the supermarket. However, John may decide to close up shop because, in analysing his weaknesses such as comparatively higher prices and a narrower range, he realises that he's too vulnerable and he should quit while the going is good. Fishing in the local dam becomes an overwhelmingly attractive alternative.

Reversing the order of SWOT analysis makes it no less effective and, as the example shows, it can form an integral part of our matrix.

The principle of irresistible temptation and tobogganing in the dark

As you will by now have realised, the matrix builds on the well-tried methodology of scenario planning. It adds a third and fourth quadrant to represent the two final stages of decision-making – option formulation and choice – after the scenarios have been compiled. For this reason, we have subtitled the book "scenario planning in *action*". It completes the loop, so to speak. Before moving on to a more detailed analysis of the four quadrants, we would like to relate one story and two quotes from a trio of internationally acclaimed and very foxy futurists. They all worked for Royal Dutch Shell which is considered the holy grail of scenario planning. Then we'll close the section with a cautionary tale.

Pierre Wack headed Shell's scenario planning department during the 1970s and acted as consultant to Anglo American's scenario team during the construction of the High Road/Low Road scenarios in the 1980s. He was assisted by Ted Newland, another scenario giant who used to work at Shell. Pierre is considered the pathfinder of scenario planning along with Herman Kahn who wrote the

1962 bestseller *On Thermonuclear War: Thinking About the Unthinkable*. One of Pierre's favourite forms of flattery was to call you a remarkable person. He was, as the following story indicates, one of the most remarkable men of all. In the mid-1970s, Pierre nominated two rules of the game governing the future of the oil business. The first rule was that the supply of oil would decline because, as Arab countries received a higher price per barrel, they wouldn't need to sell so much oil to meet their domestic commitments. The second rule was that demand for oil would continue to rise, even at higher prices, because Western countries could not put in conservation measures fast enough to reduce consumption. The key uncertainty was at what point in time the downward sloping supply curve would intersect the upward sloping demand curve. If sooner, the scenario was a second oil price shock (the first one occurred in the early 1970s when the price went from $3 to $12 a barrel). This would be caused by the market entering a "zone of anxiety" in which the "principle of irresistible temptation" prevailed. Rotterdam spot traders would see the tightening of the market and ramp the price skywards. If the intersection was later, the price would remain firm at $12. Shell had two options – base their strategy on the "second shock" scenario or on business as usual. In the event, they chose the "second shock" scenario, the oil price soared to over $30 a barrel and Shell scored mightily, moving up to pole position among the oil giants. Pierre always looked for the points of greatest leverage in terms of bang for the buck: and this was a perfect illustration.

Pierre's successor at Shell was Peter Schwartz who went on to establish the Global Business Network in California and wrote *The Art of the Long View: Planning for the Future in an Uncertain World*. Along with Pierre's two-part article in the *Harvard Business Review* of September/October, 1985 entitled "The Gentle Art of Reperceiving", this book must rate as the best in scenario literature. The memorable quote from it is: "An old Arab proverb says that he who predicts the future lies even if he tells the truth."

The third person is Arie de Geus, who was co-ordinator of group planning at Shell and has, since his retirement from Shell, concentrated on showing how managers and organisations actually learn to do new things. In a piece entitled "Planning as Learning" he made what at first blush may appear to be a surprising statement: "A child who is playing with a doll learns a great deal about the real world at a very fast pace." However, based on this principle, business executives on management courses in Europe participate in a game called Lego Serious Play. They apparently use the blocks to demonstrate in a practical way their vision for the company. Then they demolish their models and start afresh, thus learning the importance of being adaptable. Arie's point is that lengthy lectures from planners seldom lead to a change of behaviour in an audience of experienced executives. Games do and scenarios in a sense are a series of "what if" games.

Now we come to the cautionary tale. One of us (no prize for hazarding a guess!) was visiting Boston in the mid-1980s to give a guest lecture on scenario planning at the Harvard Business School. It was February and bitterly cold. The professor in charge of the course, Bruce Scott, invited Pierre Wack and the said author to his weekend retreat in the hills some miles outside the city. The countryside was covered in snow, which had been falling all week. In the evening, after a splendid meal, the host decided this was a good moment to go tobogganing down the local country lane. It was a long thin toboggan which at a pinch could accommodate three people, in this case three scenario planners. So, in the pitch dark with Bruce lighting our way with a torch, we walked to the top of the lane dragging the toboggan. Bruce sat down on it at the front, with Pierre in the middle and the said author in the rear position. Bruce pointed the torch down the lane and we set off.

Now the first rule of the game for tobogganing is that on a steep slope, when the snow is beginning to turn to ice, the toboggan will gather speed extremely quickly. Friction to retard the motion is not a factor. The second rule of tobogganing is that the route that you intend taking should be visible to the naked eye. The third rule is that at speed a torch is not effective to light up the way at night. The key uncertainty in this situation is not whether or not you are going to arrive at the bottom, but at which corner you are going to part company with the road. The options were simple: embark on this risky venture or sensibly stay at home in front of a blazing log fire nestling a nice glass of brandy. The decision was never at issue, given that male bravado rises by the power of the number of males present (in this situation it was cubed) and the quantity of wine imbibed (substantial).

The result was a sudden exit from the lane, but later than expected by the rear member of the toboggan since we made it miraculously through the early curves. None of us sustained critical injuries, as we had plunged deeply into a soft snowdrift. After dusting the snow off our clothes, we tramped back to the house with the toboggan in tow. There our spirits were revived by the log fire and brandy associated with the second option. The moral of this tale: even scenario planners have their comeuppance!

Rules of the game

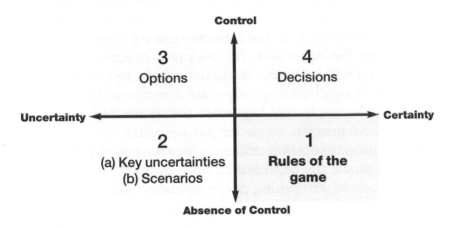

Apollo 13, Plato and chess

If you want to see how the rules of the game are applied with fox-like energy, you need do no more than microwave some popcorn, kick off your shoes, take the phone off the hook and watch *Apollo 13* on video. Your ambition to pursue the merger with another company or beat your family doctor over eighteen holes at golf will shrivel against the challenge of bringing home three astronauts hurtling out of control through space. The rules of their game include some of the most powerful and unchangeable rules in the universe – the rules of gravity, time and distance. Separated by thousands of kilometres from the Earth and faced with an unanticipated problem in their capsule, the only thing of which they are certain is a lonely, slow and horrible death if they make a mistake. They work through the matrix by starting with an examination of the astrophysical rules of the game. There'll be more on the fate of our astronauts later.

Plato said that the unexamined life is not worth living. In business, you might say that the unexamined game is not worth playing. Consider sending a team of rugby players on to a hockey field without sticks and expecting them to play hockey. They couldn't. They would neither know the rules of the game nor would they be properly equipped. Yet in business we do it all the time. We enter a game without examining the rules and the resources required to play. Worse, you will find some companies that, even in this day and age of emphasising corporate communication, keep their employees in the dark as to the nature of the game itself. Consequently, some employees pitch up wearing white flannels expecting cricket; others have studded boots on for football; the third bunch have donned headgear in anticipation of scrumming down for rugby and so on. And then the directors expect to mould an effective team out of their workforce! Whew!

But how do foxes and hedgehogs view the rules of the game? On the one hand, we believe that foxes embrace the rules and use them to gain advantage. They understand the boundaries of the game and that there are games within a game. They are like chess players who are thinking several moves ahead. On the other hand, hedgehogs can't see beyond the present. They are constantly breaking the rules of the game either through ignorance or through the misbegotten belief that while the rules apply to others, *they* can wilfully break them. And if they don't break them, they can bend them to suit themselves.

Snakes, bombs and Scottish caddies

The R&A (Royal and Ancient Golf Club of St Andrews) is the governing authority for the Rules of Golf outside the United States of America and its territories. One of the most unusual judgements the R&A Rules Committee has been asked to make in recent years concerned the dramatic experience of a golfer in Africa. As he was approaching the top of his back swing for a shot from the light rough, a dangerous snake slithered between his feet. With a fine adjustment to his downswing he delivered a fatal blow to the snake's head. Should it be counted as a stroke? After much deliberation the golfer was given a "not guilty" verdict. It was thought that the intention to strike the ball ceased at the moment he spotted the snake.

During the Second World War, many people clung to normality by continuing to play golf, and a special set of wartime rules was drawn up by Major G.L.Edsell. He generously allowed players to take shelter without penalty during gunfire or while bombs were falling. The positions of known delayed-action bombs were marked by red and white flags, which the small print added were "placed at reasonably, but not guaranteed, safe distances from the bombs". A ball moved by enemy action could be replaced. If lost or destroyed another ball could be dropped without penalty. But a player whose stroke was affected by the simultaneous explosion of a bomb or shell, or by the sound of machine-gun fire, could play another ball only under penalty of one shot.

Although we may shake our heads and chuckle at the idiosyncrasies of the game of golf that sees the rules respected and adhered to in such extremes, the fact is that in golf, as indeed in life, there are rules that are certain, cannot be broken, are out of our control and therefore should be respected. As we have already intimated, the rules of any game cannot be changed unless the relevant and recognised authority has agreed that they should. Moreover, rules are necessary: otherwise games, which are just one manifestation of organised human behaviour, would not be possible. The rules of golf will no doubt be cursed by the frustrated hacker who has had a spectacularly "off" day and single-handedly redesigned the course with his six-iron – but they *are* necessary. There was an occasion when an American tourist, playing extraordinarily bad golf at St Andrews, remarked to his caddie that this was not his usual game. With the customary dry wit of a Scot, the caddie replied: "What then, sir, is your usual game? Tennis, baseball, ten-pin bowling . . . ?"

The last story does raise an important pair of guidelines for budding entrepreneurs. First, study the rules of the game of the industry you intend going into very carefully. Does it provide a real opportunity of making money? Or could you be condemned to a life of slogging your guts out trying to get blood out of a stone? So many people do this, it's not funny. Second, ask yourself whether you have a natural ability to succeed in that sector. The last thing you want to do is stumble in because you, or your parents or your friends, thought it was a good idea at the time. It's no good being a gunslinger with a slow hand in a game where you're quick or you're dead. It may sound very obvious but at the outset the question is: "Am I in the right game – for me?"

Narrowing the cone of uncertainty

Far from being *prescriptive*, the rules of the game should be viewed as *descriptive*, as they shape the parameters within which we can operate. They show how the system ticks. Imagine the future opening up like a cone of uncertainty, as illustrated in the accompanying diagram. What the rules of the game do is to reduce that cone within reason and limit the number of outcomes. Hence, the inner cone with the three little discs on the rim (indicating possible scenarios). For instance, given the rules of soccer, you will hardly ever have a score at the final whistle as high as in a rugby game. Pierre Wack once said that, in making a good decision, it is as informative to know which futures are excluded by the rules of the game as it is to know which ones lie within the rules. In fact, a facilitator in a scenario workshop should squeeze the cone to as narrow a funnel as possible so that his group can concentrate their energy on handling the range of futures they plausibly face. Remember, business –

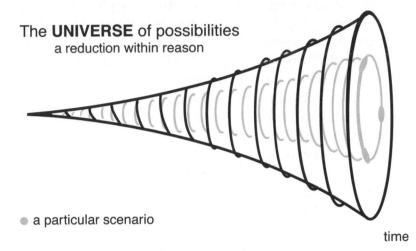

The **UNIVERSE** of possibilities
a reduction within reason

● a particular scenario

time

as well as politics – is the art of the possible. It undoubtedly causes frustration to dwell at length on the rules of the game when people are eager to discuss proposals for action. But it's like drawing back a bow. You have to make it as tight as you can before releasing the arrow. Then you have a chance of hitting the target.

Moreover, without first establishing what you don't control, you will not achieve a firm understanding of what you do control. And you may be surprised by how much you do control. For the most inspiring examples of this principle, you only have to look at invalids who lead normal lives under the harshest of circumstances. They are not restricted. On the other hand, action programmes without rules of the game preceding them are merely "wish lists" where nothing ever gets done. Often lack of money is the reason, because no-one has worked out beforehand where it is going to come from. How many anti-poverty programmes have failed for this reason? Similarly, the failure of summits, conferences and workshops to follow through on the resolutions passed at the end of the proceedings is often attributable to transgressing one simple rule: people have to go back to their jobs; they have other fish to fry. They don't have the time – especially the bigwigs. When something doesn't work or doesn't happen, the likelihood is that you're breaking some fundamental rule of human nature. Most revolutionary changes in a business organisation are like that – dreamed up in haste by consultants, only to peter out when human nature reasserts itself.

In science, of course, the laws are such that – at the macro-level – the cone of uncertainty vanishes into a straight line. Scientific equations are hard predictions that if the left-hand side is fulfilled, the right-hand side will follow. Unfortunately, as we have repeatedly stated, this clarity does not extend to the world of human affairs in general and business in particular, where an irreducible element of uncertainty will always be found. After all, we all have free will which allows us occasionally to flout the rules!

The good, the bad and the media

Depending on the outcome of your particular game, you may describe the rules as good, bad or just plain ugly. However, even the legendary Wild West – epitomised by the many "spaghetti" Westerns starring an avenging Clint Eastwood – had rules. They may have been unwritten, but they were *understood*. They were not drawn up on gleaming mahogany desks by distinguished fellows in an ancient Scottish golf club. The rules were informal and silently agreed upon, enforced by the so-called "code of the cowboy". For example, you didn't take another man's horse. But if a man cheated at poker, you were quite entitled to shoot him because you just *didn't* cheat at poker! Nor did you count your money at the table while the cards were being dealt. However, once the cards were in your hand, you had to know when to hold 'em and when to fold 'em – the golden rule of poker.

Most commentators will agree that we have come a long way since the rootin' tootin' tumbleweed-strewn saloons of the Wild West. Yet the unwritten rules still apply in another game with an equally lawless frontier: business. The first thing any new recruit should do in a company is suss out its invisible rules – if he or she wants to get on, that is. But witness the showdown between the marshall of satellite TV, Rupert Murdoch, and the football-crazy citizens of Manchester in the late 1990s. In September 1998, news broke that the world's most famous soccer club, Manchester United, had accepted a bid of £625 million from Murdoch's BSkyB to acquire the company that controlled the club. To ordinary folk, Murdoch's power and influence is almost beyond comprehension. His business game is motivated not by money, but by a desire continually to expand his formidable empire. His purchase of the rights to broadcast NFL football in the US has elevated him to the number four position among American broadcasters. It has also given him the leverage and financial clout to own superteams that play football, basketball and ice hockey in the two media capitals of the US – Los Angeles and New York. He also holds the rights to broadcast the Premier League matches in the UK. He now controls the most profitable satellite-TV operator in the world. He is also very well connected politically, numbering among his friends the British Prime Minister, Tony Blair.

You would therefore feel it legitimate to draw the conclusion that if anyone had the means to influence the rules of the game, it was the media mogul Rupert Murdoch. Moreover, he would have the support of the Labour-leaning Manchester United fans. Yet, he was stopped in his bid to add the ultimate jewel to his crown not by the BBC or the British Office of Fair Trade, but by the football supporters themselves. Under the co-ordination of SUAM (Supporters Against Murdoch) – founded within hours of the announcement of the bid – and the Football Supporters Association, a popular revolt was instigated. Fuelled by a growing concern about higher ticket prices and a fear that the transaction would endanger the "soul" of the game, the revolt spread and ultimately led to the deal falling through. In retrospect, Murdoch was obviously unaware of the unstated rule that English soccer clubs are not like American baseball teams which go automatically to the highest bidder. In Chris and Tara Brady's book *Rules of the Game*, the authors refer to the "too-fat-cat" rule: while it is permissible to be a fat cat in Britain, you can't be too fat cat. Likewise, in Murdoch's Australia, the poppies can't be too tall. In other words, don't take too many liberties with the British public: success is okay but excess isn't. Having said all that, class remains a highly influential unwritten rule governing British society; and Eton still gives you a good start in life. Murdoch didn't go to Eton.

It's all about values, stupid

Foxes have a nose for the intangible, informal, unwritten rules of the game and instinctively try to avoid overstepping the mark. In golf, foxes give short putts on the green that might have made their opponents sweat. On the cricket field, foxes will immediately walk if they know they've nicked the ball straight off their bat into the hands of a fielder. It is an informal rule of cricket that you don't wait for the umpire to give you out. Changing the occasional thud of willow against leather for the continuous shout of traders on the floor, the London Stock Exchange operated on the informal rule of "my word is my bond" for centuries. And you won't get anybody more foxy than a stockbroker. In companies, foxes never break the unwritten rule of merit, which is to choose the best person for the job irrespective of gender or colour.

Hedgehogs are not so sensitive; they have their own agendas. The classic example of a hedgehog-type blunder occurred on 1 February 1981 in a limited-overs cricket match between Australia and New Zealand. The latter required six runs to tie the game with one ball of the game remaining. The batsman facing the delivery was the Kiwi No. 11, Neil McKechnie. He had never hit a six in an international game. Even so, the Australian captain, Greg Chappell, ordered his younger brother, Trevor, to bowl a "sneak" (an underarm ball along the ground) to deprive the opposition of even the slightest chance of a tie. This he did and it was within the written rules. However, it went clean against the spirit of the game and outraged New Zealanders to the extent that they talked of scrapping diplomatic ties. In retrospect, the Chappell brothers mightily regretted the incident, going to show that the unwritten rule rules, OK!

It is for this reason that big business is regulated by statutory anti-trust and anti-monopoly bodies in places like the US and UK. Whilst there is a thicket of explicit regulations governing mergers and acquisitions, the overriding and unwritten rule is whether or not a transaction is in the "public interest" or not. The objective is that no individual or institution should come out a winner at the expense of everybody else.

The latest company to fall foul of this unwritten rule is Microsoft, which undoubtedly was *the* company of the 1990s. They were asked by the courts in America to break themselves up into two pieces, a ruling which they have managed to overturn. Yet, in the minds of many of the American public, Microsoft has got too big for its own boots and, more importantly, for the good of America. However brilliant their legal defence, they could be digging an even bigger hole for themselves in the perceptions of ordinary middle-class Americans. Bill Gates, the foxy nerd who struck it rich, could become Gates the mighty hedgehog.com. Even the second richest man in the world can have problems with his image.

This would seem an appropriate time for us to introduce the ultimate, invisible system that ought to be controlling human behaviour – the moral rules of the game. These rules can be compared to what surfers describe as "full stop rock" at the famous surfers' resort of Jeffrey's Bay in the Eastern Cape of South Africa. The rock is concealed under shallow water and, to all intents and purposes, is invisible until you hit it. Then you know all about it! The trend today is that big business – whether it likes it or not – has to subscribe to these rules, because there are activist NGO watchdogs following their every move and ready to bite if needs be. The public anyway have formed a cynical attitude towards the motivations of big business. Whenever the media break a new story, such as the Ford/Bridgestone saga where fatal accidents have been attributed to the covers of Firestone tyres fitted to Ford Explorers peeling off at speed, the damage to the company's image can be enormous and no amount of public relations spin can undo it. Unless you are seen to act quickly to remedy the problem and recompense the victims, you are in for a torrid time.

The best lesson in damage control in the recent past by a major corporate player is Coca-Cola's recall of 2,5 million bottles in Belgium in June 1999. This followed reports that children were being treated at a hospital after drinking Coke at their school. It appeared that production problems at two plants – one in Belgium and the other in France – may have been linked to this incident. Bans on the sale of Coke were imposed in several European countries while consumers in others steered away from drinking the stuff. Not only was Coca-Cola swift in implementing the recall; it also made a public apology for the incident and pledged to reimburse the medical expenses of those affected. After a fortnight, business was back to normal, proving that foxes sometimes come in the shape of a Coke bottle! Besides which, they have the fizz of the liquid inside.

Quite unfairly, foxes are perceived as creatures with plenty of guile but little moral sense. The truth is that foxes have a sensitivity to moral issues seldom demonstrated by hedgehogs who feel they are above the law. Foxes have good manners because they respect the little things in life. In this respect, what a splendid example of a fox was Fritz Schumacher, the German economist, who wrote the classic treatise *Small is Beautiful, A Study of Economics as if People Mattered*, first published in 1973. That went right against the trend in those days. Foxes are sometimes labelled as eccentrics, but they follow the old motto "manners makyth man". Similarly, foxy companies have their idiosyncrasies, but they understand that a clean, decent image is a competitive advantage these days. Moreover, they believe in human interaction. It does a lot more for improving employee morale and changing behaviour for the better than newfangled management techniques that come and go ever will.

One of the most famous articulations of the moral rules of the game is found in the Old Testament. The Ten Commandments are not only fundamental moral laws – otherwise they'd have been called the "ten guidelines" – they also form a good practical basis for running a modern society. It is interesting to note that of the ten commandments, eight prohibit certain behaviour and only two place positive demands on you. Falling into the former category are commands *not* to have other gods; worship golden idols; blaspheme; murder; commit adultery; steal; lie about your neighbour; or covet his wife, servants and possessions. In the positive category, the commands are to respect the Sabbath and honour your father and mother. In today's world where lack of spiritual values, greed, bad language, violent crime, promiscuity and rape, theft, deceit, envy, workaholism and unruly children are a sad reflection of how little we have progressed, the commandments would appear to be a solid ethical framework for hedgehogs and foxes alike. They are not sentimental or soppy. On the contrary, the commandments are as hard as "full-stop rock". For example, they are needed to stop modern evils like paedophilic rings on the Internet. Yet, they do not rule out the principal driving force of free enterprise, which is to pursue one's own interests. They merely prohibit certain shady ways of doing so. Being foxy is fine: being a wolf is not!

Islam also offers absolutely hard and fast rules of morality. Indeed, it is the unchanging nature of those rules that give Muslims a fundamentally secure basis for life and the confidence to become entrepreneurs and run foxy family businesses.

However, for those who would prefer something with less of a religious connotation, the "four-way test" read out at the beginning of Rotary Club functions concerning the things we think, say or do is a good start: (1) Is it the truth? (2) Is it fair to all concerned? (3) Will it build goodwill and better friendships? and (4) Will it be beneficial to all concerned? There's nothing amazingly original about any of these questions, but how many people – let alone companies – can answer them in the affirmative when making a decision? To the criticism that all this stuff sounds old-fashioned and prudish, our retort is that economic growth is only sustainable in the long run if there is a fair degree of trust between the governing classes and the governed; the country is peaceful and free of corruption and crime; citizens are generally healthy and free of stress; and a sense of justice prevails at large. We all talk now of working towards a civil society. Well, civility goes with the kind of values implied in the four-way test.

The old order changeth

Picture the moral rules of the game as an invisible spider web hanging in the ether, waiting to catch unsuspecting celebrities. Nothing can move a prominent individual faster from hero to zero than being caught in the web. Occasionally, a celebrity can wriggle his way out like Bill Clinton with his ingenious definition of sex. According to this definition, dimpled chads would not have counted as votes in the last presidential election. Work that one out! But the vast majority of the spider web's famous victims end up being co-cooned and forgotten.

Over time, the spider web changes shape and position. What was acceptable yesterday is no longer acceptable today. For many years in Italy, company directors oiled the wheels of the state's bureaucracy with lavish bribes. It was the done thing. Suddenly the tide turned after the intervention of an aggressive magistrate; and many a financial director of an illustrious company was left high and dry, gasping for air on the beach as his colleagues abandoned him. On a wider scale, think back to the Romans. They offered nations around them a simple choice: either volunteer to be part of the Roman Empire or be annihilated by our legions. This brutal principle of empire-building stood until the middle of the last century. But then the rule changed and invasions were no longer allowed. Iraq's Hussein and

Serbia's Milosevic were caught in the web. Now the web is closing in on dictators suspected of torturing and slaughtering their own citizens in large numbers, as well as those who siphon the nation's wealth into their foreign bank accounts. In Roman times, CNN wasn't around to film what the legions did to subjugate other nations. Now, the victims of a Western bombing raid on Baghdad are interviewed in their hospital beds. To television viewers, strong-arm tactics are unacceptable if innocent victims are a visible consequence.

In the world of commerce and industry, "corporate governance" is not just a buzz word. It is a new piece of the spider web, changing the rules of the game about how a company should be run. The positions of chairperson and CEO should no longer be vested in the same individual, as this concentrates too much power in a single pair of hands. For the sake of checks and balances, the chairperson should be nonexecutive. The major subcommittees of the board of directors should also be chaired by nonexecutive directors. Companies should issue reports on their performance in areas such as safety, health and the environment, as well as ones describing their social responsibility programmes. The traditional annual report is not comprehensive enough.

Hence, it is not the rules of the game that applied in the past that you should be considering in the first quadrant of our matrix, it is the ones that will apply in the future. Rules change. Just think of smoking! Next, it may be carbon emissions that have to be reduced in light of global warming and more frequent conditions of extreme weather. But, for a real flip-flop, you need look no further than the area of corporate strategy. Diversification was all the rage in the 1960s to reduce the risk associated with any one particular business. Now, the fund managers and market analysts want companies to focus. Stick to your knitting, go back to your core business, they say. Indeed, they want you, the company, to be the pure play, while *they* decide on the portfolio mix and diversity. Some would call it poetic justice, but of course the rules of the stock market have changed for the fund managers as well. In these days of instant information, frictionless trading and emphasis on short-term performance, selective crashes of individual shares – as opposed to the market as a whole – are becoming increasingly common. Unexpected profit warnings are a kiss of death and down goes the share by up to 50 per cent in a day. Markets generally can go up or down three to five per cent in a single session! The rules for a volatile market are very different to the ones that apply when the market is operating smoothly. Woe betide the fund manager who doesn't adjust his strategies accordingly. All this suggests that a decision which is correct today may be wrong tomorrow, should the rules change. And you have to be prepared to do things differently when the rules *do* alter. How many businesses have been turned into non-businesses by a change in the rules without the owner even being aware of it? By contrast, how many entrepreneurs have made fortunes because they were the first to spot that the rules had changed?

The general public now have a record proportion of their assets invested in the stock market, either directly in shares or through unit trusts and mutual/retirement funds. In view of this, they are going to have to become accustomed to the uncertainties associated with the left-hand side of our matrix as their wealth waxes and wanes in line with movements in the market. Equally, broader share ownership has interesting implications for the economy, because there is now a much stronger linkage between the stock market and the real economy via the so called "wealth effect": when people feel richer they spend more, and when they feel poorer they spend less. Back in the last century, shares could rise and fall and it would only affect the spending habits of the rich. Now, market volatility could influence the way the middle and lower income groups dispose of their income as well.

In preparing business scenarios, an important rule of the game to examine is the changing demography of the world as a whole, of the country in which you are based and of the market that you serve. You need a feel for this rule over the next twenty years; and, sadly nowadays, you have to include the likely impact of the HIV/AIDS epidemic and other diseases on your customer base. Probable advances in technology also feature as a prime rule of the game. They may enable your business to expand into new areas or they may threaten some of your products. Illustrating the last point is the famous story about Western Union being handed the telephone on a plate by Alexander Graham Bell. They turned him down because they thought the future still rested on telegrams and the morse code. An up-to-date example is the way CDs wiped out LPs. It would not have been smart to open an LP factory in the late 1980s! Now, despite Napster's legal woes, the Internet combined with MP3s is transforming the music industry once again. If nothing else, we are going to have virtual jukeboxes where you can listen to your favourite songs and jive the night away – using your personal computer as a record player.

A company's future competitive position vis-à-vis its rivals in the same market is very much a rule of the game. Here we can quote South African Breweries and how they saw things before the new millennium started. SAB visualised the beer market of the 21st century evolving into three leagues. The first was the premier league in which world-class companies like Anheuser Busch and Heineken were currently located with worldwide premium brands. The second league was that of national champions in which SAB, sundry British brewers and Carlsberg were represented. The third league was the niche/boutique one where specialist beers produced by European monasteries resided. Given this rule, SAB foresaw a danger for themselves in remaining in the middle league. For another rule of the game was that the middle league is vulnerable to intrusion from world-class players in the top one. The latter could – through economies of scale and selecting best practice from around the world – gradually eat up the markets of the national champions. SAB therefore had the choice to ascend into the world-class category or descend into niche businesses. They opted for ascension: this entailed a move of their head office from Johannesburg to London as the most appropriate base from which to launch their campaign for premier league status.

The "G" word

However, nothing illustrates the point of looking forwards rather than backwards better than globalisation. Before it arrived, many businesses were comfortably protected from the chilly winds of international competition by tariffs and quotas imposed on imports. Now it's open sesame: you either set standards equivalent to best practice in the rest of the world or your business dies. Globalisation is like playing golf without handicaps. The scratch player will always win. So unless you start emulating Tiger, you don't stand a chance. Thus, the globalisation rule has necessitated extremely painful adjustments to companies and societies alike – protagonists would say for the better; antagonists, who include the demonstrators that have thronged the offices of the World Bank and International Monetary Fund, would say for the worse. One thing is for sure: the nature of work and jobs is undergoing a metamorphosis which is not going to reverse itself. The two great engines of job creation for most of the last century – the public sector and big business – have shut down. In fact, globalisation has converted both of them into net job destroyers as they seek to be leaner and meaner than their next-door neighbours. That leaves medium-sized, small and micro enterprise as the area of most potential for future employment. It suggests another rule of the game for parents: their kids are going to have to be taught to be entrepreneurs during their school years if they want to find work. The accent will need to be on creativity and problem-solving rather than learning by rote. If parents really want to turn their offspring into foxes, there is no better way to do it than divide their pocket money in half and put one half into a savings account that can only be used to set up a business. The other half constitutes normal disposable income. One foxy child said to his parents that this arrangement was fine, provided they doubled the pocket money first!

Globalisation is also transforming the agricultural industry in the world today. If you're a commodity farmer in maize, wheat, cotton, cattle or sheep, the new rule of the game is that you have to achieve economies of scale on a par with world-class agri-businesses in Western countries. In order to do this, size becomes critical. Farms are therefore merging or are being bought out, with the consequence that land ownership is becoming more concentrated. Now is this a good thing, when another rule of the game is that land is a very emotive issue? We seem to have conflicting rules. On the other hand, dividing up large farms into smaller ones to satisfy land hunger isn't going to work either. Anybody banking on commodity prices in real terms rising to assist such a process is in for disappointment, because the world has a permanent surplus of commodities – that is another rule of the game. The alternative is to focus on speciality products or move out of conventional farming altogether by going into bed-and-breakfasts, game farming and trophy hunting, breeding disease-free animals, etc. One farmer near Mafikeng is now the largest parrot exporter in Africa! However, there is an answer to the thorny issue of world-class efficiency versus wider land ownership. It involves lateral thinking, which lies at the heart of our matrix. We'll explain it after we have covered "win-win" outcomes in the next section.

For now, though, a final word on globalisation, having just dealt with the moral rules of the game. It is in the nature of competition that the gap between the winners and the losers widens. Remember the maxim: "To the victor go the spoils." Globalisation at the moment could be renamed Americanisation because America sucks in the brains from the rest of the world. Indeed, America can cherry-pick talented Third World doctors, teachers, engineers and computer programmers at will, unintentionally doing more harm to the countries exporting these precious skills than by declaring war on them. The end result is that everybody regards America as the winner. This belief feeds on itself and makes America even more powerful in the global economic game and the rest less powerful. As an aside, the same "halo effect" applies to Murdoch's former acquisition target – Manchester United. As the richest and most successful soccer club in England's Premier League, it automatically attracts the best and the brightest football stars. So guess what – it is the odds-on favourite to win the league yet again. How boring for the fans who support other clubs!

However, if the gap between the haves and the have-nots widens to a totally unreasonable extent, then another rule of the game kicks in, which is injustice. Nothing could be more expressive of this rule than the words of a young Brazilian woman at a recent conference held in Porto Alegre in Brazil: "Can we not imagine a better world than this? Where the air will be free from the poison of fear of insecurity? Where the TV set is not the most important member of the family? Where food and communication will not be commodities because the right to eat and talk to each other are human rights? Where justice and liberty, Siamese twins condemned to live apart, shall again be conjoined back-to-back?" When the majority of people in any situation feel that injustice has gone too far like this young woman, they start a rebellion. This would not be in America's interest. So America has to optimise between two rules of the game – the globalisation one and the injustice one. But this is precisely what foxes are about. They don't pursue any one rule of the game as an ideology to the utter exclusion of all the others. Hedgehogs do!

In the business world, rules constantly clash. For example, one rule says that you ought to maximise profits for shareholders, while another says you should make a permanent contribution towards the communities where you operate. No clearer example of this tussle exists than the drug companies and their quandary over the prices they should charge for HIV/AIDS drugs in developing countries. But banks are next in line. They are coming under increasing pressure to behave like they did in the good old days when the bank manager was a pillar of the community and made credit available to people who would not normally get it. Against this, shareholders are demanding that banks concentrate on their highest value-adding activities such as servicing large corporate clients and high net worth individuals. Somehow a compromise solution has to be found.

Curves of pleasure and pain

In every competitive sport, you have a result involving winners and losers – in other words a "win-lose" outcome. Where the gains exactly match the losses, science calls this a "zero-sum" game. Physical laws like the one relating to the conservation of mass and energy are zero-sum: if mass or energy disappears from one part of the universe, an equivalent amount will reappear, maybe in a different form, somewhere else. Thus mass and energy can be transferred but the total amount in the universe will remain the same.

Life can also have win-lose, zero-sum outcomes. We have already mentioned sport but gambling falls into the same category. Take a poker game between two players: if one player wins a million dollars, the other must have lost it. CEOs often regard business as a zero-sum game. They only feel they've won if somebody else is licking his wounds because he's lost. In some circumstances – like tendering for a large project – they are right. But there are other outcomes, life being more subtle than sport or science.

Imagine an all-out nuclear war between two nations where mutual destruction is not only assured but actually materialises. With devastated cities on both sides of the border, that is definitely a "lose-lose" outcome. You can also have " win-win" situations in human relationships created by love, friendship, parenthood or the pursuit of knowledge. When two people fall in love, you don't normally call one a winner and the other a loser unless you have a deep disregard for one of them. Good teachers can have synergistic relationships with their classes so that everybody at the conclusion of the term is happy and inspired. Stephen Covey in his book *The 7 Habits of Highly Effective People* maintains that the only viable outcome in the long run to a negotiation is win-win or else the parties should walk away. The reason is that a win-lose outcome will fester in the mind of the losing party and gradually erode his enthusiasm for the deal. Since the winning party may well be relying on the continued co-operation of the losing party, he will ultimately lose in the end as well.

This reasoning leads to the enunciation of three of the

most important unwritten rules of the game: (1) virtually all decisions about the future involve a judgement of risk versus reward, because life is a risky business, (2) in most situations decision makers must take into account the reasoning and state of mind of other decision makers, and (3) even where there is conflict of interest, the outcome must be beneficial to both parties for the decision to stick. These three rules apply as much to companies as they do to individuals. Game theory, which was originally developed in a book entitled *The Theory of Games and Economic Behaviour* by John von Neumann and Oskar Morgenstern and published in 1944, expands on these rules. Let us begin with a diagram that we have christened "curves of pleasure and pain":

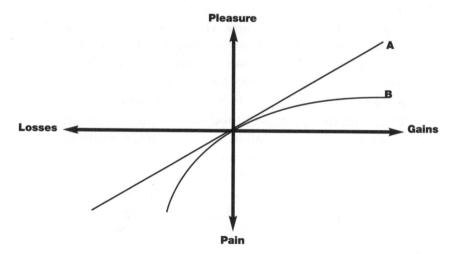

The horizontal axis denotes gains and losses. These could take various forms, but for the purposes of this book we'll denominate them as monetary gains and losses. The vertical axis measures the pleasure or pain of an individual as he makes gains or suffers losses. It is clear that Person A is either very rich or has an inveterate gambling streak. If he wins or loses the same amount, the graph tells you that however much that amount is, the pleasure and the pain are equally balanced against one another. Bunker Hunt, the American billionaire, was once asked how he felt about losing a billion dollars on the silver market. His response: "You win some. You lose some."

Person B is more like most of us – of modest means and risk-averse. On the one hand, the pain associated with a loss rises exponentially beyond a certain amount of money. On the other hand, the pleasure linked to a monetary gain starts levelling out when the sum becomes ridiculous and individual B doesn't know what to do with it other than leaving it to the kids who will promptly be spoilt by it. If you can't conceive of ever having too much money for any addition to become irrelevant, then your curve on the right-hand side of the diagram rises in a straight line!

The left-hand side of the curve is, however, completely different if you're a person of B's temperament. Beyond a certain amount, it doesn't matter what your attitude is: the pain of a loss will eventually outweigh the pleasure of a gain. To illustrate this point, think of a coloured disc where 70 per cent of the area is coloured blue and 30 per cent red. Would you be prepared to spin the disc on the basis that if the pointer was on blue when the disc came to rest, you would win a million dollars? But if it was on red, you'd lose it, in which case your house, your spouse and your car go up in smoke. Supposing 99 per cent of the disc was blue and one per cent red, would you review the situation and risk it? And what if we said you could only lose a hundred thousand dollars on red but still make a million dollars on blue? Mathematics says you're an idiot if you don't take any of these bets; but then the rules of mathematics do not incorporate human psychology – the rules of real life do. Curve B also explains why most people get more conservative as they get older. They don't want to lose the assets or reputation they've accumulated. Meanwhile, the young have nothing to lose: they can be radical.

Curve B has relevance in quite different contexts. Earlier we referred to the capacity of the human intellect to play tug-of-war with opposing ideas. On the emotional side, we have mixed feelings about people and things. For example, when we help ourselves to a particularly generous portion of chocolate cake, we experience the direct pleasure of consuming something wonderfully rich; but we also feel pangs of guilt about our lack of self-restraint. Hence, we yo-yo up and down the curve with dietary schizophrenia.

Curve B also highlights the danger of narcotics. The addict will seek bigger highs (gains) from harder drugs as he runs into the law of diminishing pleasure on the right of the chart. Sadly too, his increasing dependency on drugs means that he loses control over his life – options and decisions become irrelevant. In addition, the curve explains why relief from physical pain like toothache and psychological pain like anxiety over health can cause such intense pleasure: you're moving very quickly up the steep side of the curve on the left. It also supports the theory that the most effective way to increase the general happiness of a nation is to target the ultra-poor and improve their quality of life. In essence, you are giving them a leg up the left-hand side of the curve by reducing their daily misery. Jeremy Bentham, the philosopher and social reformer who founded the philosophy of "utilitarianism", would nod his head in approval. In his major work, *Principles of Morals and Legislation* published in 1789, he stated that the object of all legislation should be "the greatest happiness for the greatest number". He was also a fox because he maintained that his principle of "utility" was best served by allowing every man to pursue his own interests unhindered by restrictive legislation.

Given that Curve B represents the psychology of the average person, Covey's proposition that outcomes to negotiations should be win-win to have any chance of lasting a long time appears valid. For if you negotiate something that is very advantageous to yourself but equally disadvantageous to the other party, he or she is going to feel far sicker about it than you are going to have reason to rejoice. Their motivation to undermine the deal is therefore going to be stronger than your wish to make it stand. You might have good lawyers on your side to draft an unbreakable agreement which can hold up in any court, but what you don't control is the attitude of the other party during the period that the agreement is implemented. You have to accept that the rules of the game in the mind of the other person may be different to your own and worthy of consideration. Rules can clash and then you have to compromise. This brings us back to the land issue raised earlier. Perhaps the way you satisfy all parties is to have bigger, more competitive farms, but then convert them into companies with a wide range of shareholders including the farmer and the employees on the farm. That way, land ownership becomes diffused. Maybe you then float the farm on the stock exchange. Who knows? The sky's the limit!

Implicit in Curve B is another unwritten rule of human behaviour: a reluctance to tinker with the status quo. Nobody is going to jump from the known and certain to the unknown and uncertain unless the known and certain is already extremely unpleasant and painful. Again the logic is simple. The unknown and uncertain offers mixed chances of gain as well as loss for the prospective jumper, and the potential pleasure associated with a gain is outweighed by the risk of major pain associated with a loss. In normal circumstances, therefore, the inclination is do nothing but stay put in familiar territory: it is the preferable option over potential oblivion, no matter what the upside. To use that overworked expression, to shift a person's paradigm or a nation's mind-set requires the affected party to have a shock to the system (not smart) or develop an understanding of what may lie on the other side before the shock happens (smarter). That's why scenarios are so useful: by offering a glimpse of the possible, they act as a catalyst to achieve the leap of understanding necessary for movement. The people of Northern Ireland and Israel need positive scenarios of what their countries could be like if they laid aside centuries of religious animosity. Then they might find one another and move to higher ground. Incidentally, inspirational tales of the past can often achieve the same result. The film *Erin Brockovich* tells the story of how a sassy, young miniskirted mother took up the cause of an American community, and won a legal case involving contaminated water against a gigantic power utility. It sent a powerful message: when ordinary people put their minds to it, they can do extraordinary things and make a difference. It also helped that the movie starred the Oscar-winning actress with the radiant smile, Julia Roberts!

Sometimes, however, the choice is between the lesser of two evils and showing people that if they don't do something which prima facie looks against their interest, there is a worse scenario waiting in the wings. For instance, you don't normally hand money over to a stranger for nothing in return. But if that stranger happens to say "your money or your life" and presses a cocked pistol against your temple, you *do* hand the money over. The alternative is worse! Dick Turpin, the famous eighteenth-century English highwayman, used this technique very effectively till he was hanged in York in 1739.

Finally, Curve B has an intriguing feature. If the time frame on the left or the right is a date sometime in the future, we discount the losses or gains because they mean less to us. For example, if the adverse effects of smoking or HIV/AIDS were felt immediately, people would be more averse to risking their lives on the immediate gratification involved in smoking a cigarette or having unsafe sex. Equally, monetary gains in the future aren't worth as much as cash in the bank now. But the area where our natural habit of discounting the future creates a real blind spot is the environment. For the beneficial impact of making sacrifices in our current lifestyle may only be felt in a few generations' time. And as some wag put it: "Why should we bother about the next generation? They have never done anything for us." Alas, the short-sightedness highlighted by this observation is becoming more relevant by the day.

It takes two to tango

This brings us to the celebrated example of the "prisoner's dilemma", as formulated by the mathematician Albert Tucker. Two men – let's call them Bill and Ben – are arrested for robbery. They are refused bail and isolated from one another in separate cells. However, the evidence is circumstantial as there are no hard witnesses. It requires one or other of them to confess for the charge of robbery to stick. Otherwise, they will be charged with carrying concealed weapons at the time of their arrest – an offence which carries a considerably lighter sentence. Both know the consequences of their decision to confess or remain silent. If they both confess, they will both get a five-year sentence; if neither confesses, they will both get one year for carrying a concealed weapon; and if one confesses while the other does not, the confessor will go free and the one who remains silent will get twenty years.

What is the best option for each prisoner? If Bill cannot trust Ben, it is arguably best for him to confess in order to limit his downside to five years at worst and zero at best.

Ben's reasoning must be the same. So, as untrusting individuals, they should both confess and get five years. If, however, they are members of the Mafia and have taken the oath of *omerta* (silence), then it pays for each of them to remain silent and go to jail for one year for the lesser offence.

The dilemma comes in when Bill and Ben are just friends. They are taken to separate interrogation cells without having any chance to compare stories or plan a strategy. The police tell Bill that Ben has already confessed. Bill has to decide whether the police are telling the truth or lying. Is Ben a friend or a double-crosser? The horns of the dilemma are very pointed and sharp for Bill.

There is no logical and satisfactory answer to this conundrum. Depending upon his personal risk profile and regard for Ben, Bill will either play safe and confess to the robbery; or take the plunge and remain silent. The intriguing thing is that this type of dilemma is repeated again and again in real life. Politicians make this judgement call whenever they have something to cover up. Should they rely on their colleagues to keep silent during the probe, in which case the cover-up option offers the best way out. Or should they tell the truth at the outset and take the rap? The problem in the cover-up option is that if they are wrong about their colleagues and the truth surfaces, they are in for the high jump. The cover-up becomes the issue as opposed to the original misdemeanour.

Here's another illustration from the real world. If I'm a grocer pondering on cutting the prices of my fruit and vegetables, the big question is whether other grocers in the neighbourhood will follow suit. If they do, every grocer will be worse off; and if they don't, I will grab their customers so I'll be better off and they will suffer. Perhaps we should instead form a cartel and fix the price of fruit and vegetables for the entire neighbourhood, with the added benefit that it is extremely unlikely that any individual grocer will break ranks and do to me what I'm thinking of doing to him. But that's precisely why cartels in most countries are illegal, because they are established for the benefit of the producers and at the expense of the consumers. It's only if you are an international cartel like OPEC that you'll get away with it. So, generally speaking, open competition is enshrined in law and the pricing dilemma that we've just alluded to persists in every player's mind.

The arms race, which seems to have somewhat abated, once posed the same dilemma to the two superpowers – America and Russia. If I developed a nuclear weapon superior to yours, I was at an advantage. If, however, you responded by creating a new generation of weapon which equated with mine, then neither of us were better off militarily – but we were sure worse off financially. Sense now seems to prevail on both sides; but don't rule out America exploiting Russia's precarious financial position to have another go at achieving military superiority. "Son of Star Wars" is reported to be on the drawing board.

We've already mentioned the three rules of the game that flow from these examples in the first paragraph on page 70. Nonetheless, it is worth re-emphasising that no company is an island, as is assumed in many a strategic plan. You have to play scenarios on the responses of the competition to any action you intend to take – before taking it. For example, if you decide to merge with another company to become a larger entity, then two of your competitors may decide to combine into an even larger one. Vicious and virtuous circles also display the same feedback principle, this time with your customers. Hike your prices too much and your customers disappear so that you have to hike them even more to maintain your revenue. Lower your prices and you may attract more customers than you anticipated, in which case you can lower them even more. As Isaac Newton said, for every action there is a reaction. Hence, there is no point in waltzing into a boardroom with a proposal, entering into negotiations on a contract or presenting a sales pitch to potential customers unless you've worked through the range of reactions which are outside your control. The penalty, should you not do this homework, may be an undignified exit with arms flailing and a bruised ego. Not worthy of a fox.

Key uncertainties

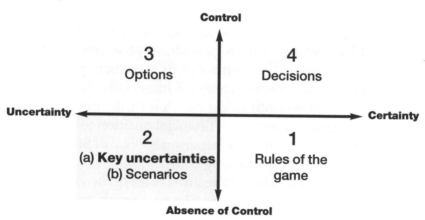

"Houston, we have a problem"

There's a saying among science-fiction buffs: "The meek shall inherit the Earth; the rest of us are going to the stars." One or two celebrity oddballs, like *Star Trek* creator Gene Rodenberry, decided to take the latter half of the statement literally. Before they died, they organised to have their ashes launched into the inky blackness of space. And there they are, orbiting forever. However, for the vast majority of us, the reality is that – in life and in death – we physically remain part of this Earth. Well, that's not entirely true. Among us are the lucky ones blessed with the right stuff, who blast off into space on quests which help us learn more about what is out there beyond the gravitational confines of this "pale blue dot" (Carl Sagan's phrase).

We travel into space because the conquest of mountains and seas has made it one of the last frontiers full of enticing unknowns. We go there because we don't know what's out there. For this reason any space journey is fraught with uncertainty and danger. The astronauts and their thousands of support personnel have to rely on what they do know, which is miniscule compared to what they don't know. Add to this their faith in the computers and other technical equipment involved in their flight, and you realise they're taking one heck of a gamble.

Back in the days of the Apollo missions, NASA enthusiastically hurled human beings at the moon at the speed of a bullet. They were exceptionally proud of their technologies – almost as proud as the builders of the *Titanic*. This ended abruptly soon after the Apollo 13 space vehicle leapt from the Kennedy Space Centre in Florida on April 11, 1970. John Swigert, Fred Haise and Jim Lovell were at the controls of what was essentially a tall tin can boasting the same computing power as a modern-day scientific calculator!

Fifty-six hours into the Apollo 13 mission an explosion on board sent the power readings haywire. At that instant, all the certainties of the mission disappeared as the crew were confronted with an emergency situation for which they hadn't been trained. The reaction of the mission commander on board, Jim Lovell, was the now famous quote "Houston, we have a problem". Upon investigation, the problem was far bigger than they anticipated. One of the oxygen tanks had exploded, resulting in an almost complete loss of capability to generate power and to provide water or oxygen to the crew. The NASA officials immediately accepted that the mission to the moon had to be scrapped and everything had to be done to bring the crew home. What was uncertain was – how?

Let's break for a minute and look at possible reactions to the discomfort of suddenly being thrust into a sea of uncertainty. The typical hedgehog reaction would be to rush back to its hole in the ground, curl itself into a ball and hope the problem would sort itself out. The reaction of a fox would be to look for the main influencing factors, see how they could be used to advantage and, in so doing, begin to cope with the new situation. With necessary apologies to Neil Armstrong, this crossing-over from the right-hand side of the matrix (certainty) to the left-hand side (uncertainty) requires one small step for a fox but one giant leap for hedge-hog-kind.

At NASA ground control, the next step was decidedly foxy – to look for the main driving forces of the situation by drawing on the multiple perspectives of some of the finest brains in the space business. Unlike the rugged gung-ho frontiersmen of the Wild West, the heroes of this frontier were teams of scientists with pocket calculators and slide rules; there were no laptops in those days! Very little was known about the effects of an explosion like this on the craft and crew, so you can imagine the list of uncertainties this situation offered: How was the craft damaged? How long would the power last? How long would the oxygen last? Could the power be restored? Would the craft start falling apart? Would the explosion affect the craft's trajectory, sending it into outer space? If the astronauts managed to head the craft back towards Earth, would the command and lunar modules be able to detach from one another? Would the damage prevent the craft from re-entering the Earth's atmosphere? What were the dangers of another explosion?

What was the quickest route to get home? And what were the realistic odds of getting the astronauts back home? Because no-one was prepared for a situation like this, the chasm between the old certainties and the new uncertainties might have seemed unbridgeable.

However, there is a continuum between certainty and uncertainty, just as there is between factors inside and outside of our control. By studying the uncertain, we may be able to break it down into elements of greater and lesser risk, of greater and lesser predictability. In the same way, between absolute control and absence of control lies the middle ground of influence and persuasion. Hence, we can travel inwards and outwards along the two principal axes of our matrix. Which is why studying the Apollo 13 mission is so fascinating. It offers us a perfect example of how people in a situation of extreme stress are still able to establish and analyse the key uncertainties, so that a sensible range of options can be mounted against what the future throws at us.

As the name suggests, key uncertainties are those variables most relevant to a particular situation and with the highest impact potential, either as an opportunity or a threat. They therefore drive the design of possible scenarios. In this regard, where a scenario planning forum raises many uncertainties, it is important that the number is whittled down to a few pivotal ones: namely the ones on which the scenarios pivot like a see-saw. For example, both of us have recently been facilitating workshops to produce scenarios which are relevant in the war against poverty in South Africa. Quite independently, both workshops chose the process through which national development strategies are implemented – will they be driven in a top-down fashion from the centre or be shaped by community demands from the bottom up? – as a pivotal uncertainty. This led to the fashioning of a third alternative: grassroots-driven development with co-ordination from on high in those areas where real value can be added.

In the 1980s, most global scenario teams selected the relationship between America and Russia as a pivotal uncertainty – would the arms race continue or would there be détente? Times change and, with the collapse of the Soviet Union, the nineties were dominated more by uncertainties in the world financial and economic systems. The "noughties", as the present decade is known, continues to be dominated by these uncertainties, which now include the tremors in the American economy. Interestingly, as far as single-business scenarios are concerned, a recent exercise selected the attitude of central banks to their gold holdings as the pivotal uncertainty for the gold market in the foreseeable future. The banks still hold over 30 000 tons of the precious metal in their vaults, which is around a quarter of the gold ever extracted from the Earth's crust. With current demand for gold approximately matched by mine supply and jewellery and investment bars which have been melted down and recycled, the banks only have to dribble a small amount of their stock onto the market every year to ruin it. On the other hand, if they ever lose confidence in holding paper currencies like the dollar, sterling, euro and yen as their reserves and add to their gold holdings, the bulls would have a field day. As one gold expert wryly observed: "The gold price can go up or down but not necessarily in that order!" Moving to the world of black gold or petroleum, the pivotal uncertainty must be not whether but when and in what form new rules will come into force to reduce carbon emissions. The second Earth Summit in Johannesburg in 2002 may be the moment of truth.

In the case of Apollo 13, ground control and crew concluded that the two key uncertainties were oxygen supply to the crew and power supply to the craft. Without oxygen the crew would die, and without power the craft wouldn't get back home.

Wild cards

Key uncertainties are factors which we have positively identified, but we don't know which way they're going to go. However, there are also other factors that we are only dimly aware of. They may represent opportunities or threats but they can't be part of any official analysis because they're too vague or too far away on the horizon. We call them "wild cards", and the best way to capture them is to exercise the right-hand side of the brain, associated with creativity, as opposed to the left-hand side, associated with spatial awareness and analysis. It is accepted by most psychologists that men are left-hemisphere dominant, whereas women lean towards the right. This suggests that women are always in their right minds! Therefore, when analysing situations that are fraught with uncertainties and have no established patterns on which to base solutions, it is often the fairer sex who contribute the more dynamic scenarios. They have a knack for picking the really surprising outcomes or UUs – unknown unknowns – as opposed to the KUs or known unknowns.

To get a better feel for the way-out nature of wild cards, let's return to the cosmos and ask "what happened before the Big Bang?" For, given the expansion of the universe, it is a fair assumption that *something happened* and that there was some form of starting point from which the universe originated. Modern science has arrived, through our knowledge of the nature of space, time and gravitation, at the same conclusion as the fifth-century Christian saint, Augustine of Hippo (don't ask), who claimed that the world was made "not *in* time, but simultaneously *with* time". In plain speaking: nothing happened before the Big Bang because there was no "before". Time only started *with* the Big Bang. Thus speculation on the causes of the Big Bang and what happened preceding it can only produce the wildest of wild cards. We have to accept the unanswerability of some questions, even though our imagination impels us to explore for an answer.

A mid-1980s global scenario study incorporated the following wild card: "Surprisingly, the one thing that terrifies Japan is the possibility of a devastating earthquake during the scenario period." The earthquake happened at Kobe in early 1995 and proved that natural disasters are an ever-present danger. However, you can have wild cards on a more personal basis. Think of the strain of planning your young son's birthday party. He wants to invite twenty of his friends to play a series of games in a public park. What are the key uncertainties in determining the success of the party – those factors you know you don't know? Will it rain? How many of his friends will arrive on the day? Will you have enough food and drink when you have in fact bought enough provisions for an army? But the wild card you don't know you don't know is that the public park has been selected by a visiting chapter of the Hell's Angels as a stopover for their breakfast run. And that's really wild.

Wow, that was close!

We move from screaming unruly children in a public park to the screams of men on the fields of battle. Key uncertainties are an integral part of warfare. In his thoughtful treatise on military science, *Strategy and Compromise,* the distinguished naval historian Admiral Samuel Elliot Morrison makes the point that in the quest to know as much as possible about the enemy, military advisers and strategists employ intelligence gathering that is never complete and is often misleading. For example, the information of an enemy's strength and intentions may well be incorrect. The generals who play scenarios of the battle that lies ahead and make the final decisions know that the information at hand has tremendous gaps, but anything is better than nothing. Military decisions are therefore based on what is known and what is known to be unknown. If a wild card then emerges out of the blue – like the enemy having a new and vastly superior weapon – then the general who has a sixth sense, or a fox's instinct, might still snatch victory from the jaws of defeat. In warfare, admits Admiral Morrison, mistakes which the top brass like to call "strategic errors" are inevitable. He says: "Other things being equal, the side that makes the fewer strategic errors wins the war."

Historians only now tell us how close we came to an all-out nuclear war in October 1962 because America and Russia at times completely misread the other's position. Earlier that year Cuba, convinced that the Americans were about to attack them, had asked for extra military aid from the Russians. The latter responded by sending missiles and building missile bases on the island capable of launching nuclear strikes on American cities. In October, President John Kennedy learnt about this and ordered a naval blockade to stop further shipment of Russian arms. He then demanded that all missiles and missile bases be removed from the island. The world held its breath for a week before Russian Premier Nikita Krushchev agreed to the demand in return for an American pledge that they wouldn't attack Cuba. The blockade was then lifted. What recent analysis of the archival material has shown is that, despite both sides having formidable intelligence networks, each leader was being given woefully incorrect information on how his counterpart was thinking. So we nearly blundered into a nuclear war. But ask yourself: how often do you make decisions based on a perfect knowledge of all the facts? Admit it – the answer is seldom, if ever. Uncertainties are woven into life and weighing them up should be second nature to anybody who wants to make the best of a situation. The second quadrant of the matrix cannot be sidestepped.

We have now come full circle back to the question of the fate of the crew of the Apollo 13. Did the combined problem-solving talents of the team on the ground and in space steer the astronauts through the stormy seas of uncertainty back to dry land? Were the craft and the crew destroyed by the crushing deceleration forces and searing heat during re-entry? Or would they skip off the atmosphere and out into space to become, in Commander Jim Lovell's words, "a monument to the US space programme"? The answer to these questions depends on whether or not the key uncertainties that they identified helped them paint useful scenarios which ultimately led them to consider the most likely options and make the most effective decisions. No offence: you'll have to read on to see if there was a happy ending.

Scenarios

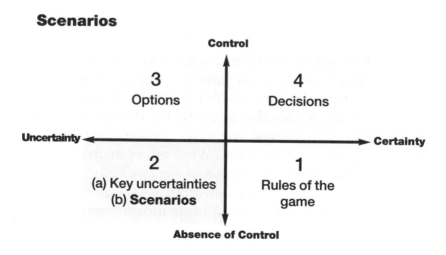

If they were still alive today, Jacob and Wilhelm Grimm would have been brilliant at writing scenarios. You may recall from your childhood that these two German brothers produced a collection of some of the most colourful and enduring fairy tales of all time – notably Snow White, Cinderella, Sleeping Beauty and Little Red Riding Hood. In the early part of the nineteenth century when they wrote these tales, multinational companies did not exist and scenario planning was not a paid occupation. Now they would be wined and dined by some of the most powerful foxes in business, looking for stories to enthral the young and old alike in their organisations; or maybe J.K.Rowling would be author of choice because of Harry Potter's rise to fame. It is not a coincidence that the book that has recently topped the New York nonfiction bestsellers' list for a long time employs the Grimm technique. It is entitled *Who Moved My Cheese?* by Dr Spencer Johnson. The story is about mice and little people and their different behaviour when their current stockpile of cheese in a maze is exhausted and they have to go in search of new cheese. It is just as enchanting as Cinderella but delivers a powerful message of how to view change as an opportunity rather than a threat.

Scenarios are stories about possible futures. Many hedgehogs in business confuse the term "scenario" with a forecast or prediction of a single future. Nothing could be further from the truth. Scenarios are, in fact, multiple pathways into a future that is unknown. While constrained by the rules of the game and driven by the key uncertainties, they should evoke the same feelings as a really good novel. Each scenario must have a simple, vivid theme which is logically consistent in itself, but differs materially from the other scenarios in the set. It must have a compelling title which enters the common vocabulary of the audience being addressed. The title should conjure up the image of the scenario without the need for the text to be read. There must not be too many scenarios, as the human mind is only capable of thinking in three dimensions. For this reason and because a prime objective of scenario work is to reduce the complex to the easily understandable, we advocate two or three scenarios (four at the very outside) for any particular situation. Only pure mathematicians can think in four or more dimensions!

However, let's go back to first principles and the Oxford English Dictionary. It defines a scenario as "a sketch or outline of the plot of a play, giving particulars of the scenes, situations, etc.". An alternative meaning taken from a dictionary of music is "an Italian term, meaning a sketch of the scenes and main points of an opera libretto, drawn up and settled preliminary to filling in the detail". Obviously, Italian composers used to peddle scenarios around well-heeled, music-loving bankers in the hope of raising money for a full production before they wasted too much effort on the score. The first known use of scenarios in a connection outside the creative arts and inside the more clinical world of science came from the sociologist, novelist and screenwriter Leo Roysten. He suggested to a group of physicists, who were searching for a name for alternative descriptions of how satellites might behave, that they call them "scenarios". He explained that this was the term used in the film industry to describe the outlines of future films. It seems fitting, therefore, to examine the scenarios that must have been playing in the minds of the crew of Apollo 13 and their helpers to get them back home.

When the proverbial hits the fan

Ever had the feeling that you're always in it and it's just the level that changes? After the on-board explosion, the crew of Apollo 13 were so far in it they needed chin-high waders! Their situation called to mind Murphy's law: "Everything that can go wrong will go wrong" and O'Brien's variation: "Murphy was an optimist". As one problem was solved, another one arose. To summarise their predicament: an explosion had destroyed a vital oxygen supply virtually robbing the command and lunar modules of power and the crew of water and limiting the supply of oxygen. In order to conserve power, the three-man crew had to move from the main navigational command module to the two-man lunar module designed only to travel to the moon's surface and back to the command module. They could only return to the command module just before splashdown.

Moreover, the explosion came after the craft had made its mid-course correction out of an immediate-return-to-Earth trajectory. So it was committed to travelling into an orbit of the moon and couldn't simply hitch a ride in the form of a direct trajectory back to Earth. The two craft, although attached, were incompatible in certain ways – the lunar module navigational system was not designed for getting back to Earth and the square canisters used to remove carbon dioxide from the command module did not fit into the round openings of the lunar module environmental system.

Without the ability to navigate, they had no hope of getting home. If carbon dioxide wasn't removed, the crew would asphyxiate. Power was needed to steer the craft: yet power was all but nonexistent. The power that remained needed to be conserved and so all but the essential requirements were cut. When the power was cut, the temperature dropped. When the temperature dropped, condensation formed on all the electrical circuitry, posing the danger of arcing and complete failure when it came time to power-up. All in all, the crew were up to their necks in it.

To follow up on our fan analogy: prima facie it would

seem that, when the proverbial hits the fan, it will not be distributed evenly and therefore no predictable pattern can be discerned. You can bet, however, that all concerned on the craft and in Houston went through the type of thinking process embedded in our matrix to narrow down the range of possible dispersion patterns. They examined the rules of the game, which mainly comprised the laws of physics; they selected two key uncertainties, namely the availability of power and oxygen; and they formulated various scenarios of the likely outcomes. Seeing that they didn't know how much power was available and they didn't know how long they could survive in the face of carbon dioxide build-up and lack of water, this all might sound airy-fairy and contrived. Which is why the Brothers Grimm would be pretty handy here! But it gave them a better clue to the options open to them and the best course of action. You will notice below that the first two scenarios on offer were utterly negative. Yet, they had good education value by informing the team as to what they should do to *minimise* the chance of either of these scenarios materialising.

The first scenario was "Close but No Cigar". Assuming they didn't have enough power to get back to Earth, they could still effectively control the carbon dioxide and conserve water and food. They wouldn't die immediately. They would hover agonisingly close to Earth until gradually and slowly they would starve to death or die of thirst. The second scenario was "Tin Tomb". Assuming they had enough power to get back to Earth, their survival mechanisms could fail them before they got there. They would be DOA (dead on arrival) with the command module being converted into a very expensive body bag. The third and positive scenario was "Sweet as Apple Pie". Assuming they had enough power to get back to Earth and their survival mechanisms remained intact, they would arrive to a hero's welcome and have apple pie with the president on the White House lawn.

We know what you're thinking: even if the astronauts were allergic to apples, they would focus on the last scenario to help them formulate their options. But that misses the whole point of scenario planning. It is only by studying all three scenarios simultaneously and looking at what you want to achieve as well as what you want to avoid that you get a feel for *all* the options. In the extreme case of life and death, we have a natural tendency anyway to do all this in the blink of an eye. It is when our lives are not at stake, and there is no emergency, that the error of concentrating on only the desired future creeps in. Take the hockey-stick projection so beloved in many companies. Like the *Nike* swoosh, it accepts a trough in the short term, but a market soaring to infinity thereafter. To adapt Keynes's famous quote, in the long term we are all optimistic! But Pollyanna would not have survived at the controls of Apollo 13.

Negotiating the rapids with the wisdom of Wack

The point we want to make from the previous narrative is that the uncertainties of a situation can be built on to give you a chance of success. There is a logic to identifying the two key uncertainties that would have the greatest impact on your business, life or situation at hand; but these uncertainties need to be translated into scenarios to give you a vision of your options. In other words, the bridging mechanism to get you from the key uncertainties to the options available is the set of scenarios or stories – the more vivid, the more contrasting but underpinned by logic, the better. This will encourage you to think the unthinkable and identify opportunities you didn't even think were there.

Problem: just when you need the Brothers Grimm for your next scenario planning session, you realise that they lived in the early nineteenth century. So where do you find the talent for story-telling? An answer: multiple perspectives from inside your own backyard. The diversity of knowledge and insight of different people within a company can provide the richness of material to develop scenarios. And it needn't just be your intellectual top guns. Encouraging ordinary people to engage in more creative and divergent thinking has the added advantage for a company of promoting expression and helping people to converse. It is this very harnessing of diversity and encouraging of creativity within groups and individual frames of mind that equip people to dream up scenarios of an unusual nature and then expand on the range of options necessary for decision-making. As Peter Schwartz said: "Scenario-making is intensely participatory, or it fails."

Imagine you and your staff are on a corporate outward bound course. You arrive at the bank of a wide river, and there's a rowing boat in front of you with which to cross the river. After a quick bout of team-building and strategic planning, you as the leader set the objective: to get to *that* specific tree on the other side. After examining your options, you work out the specific strengths of each member of your team to deal with the task at hand. Roles are delegated and, with a blood-curdling war cry, you and your team launch yourselves into the river and paddle like mad to get to that tree. Moments later you are swept downstream by the river's powerful current that you didn't know about and factor into the equation. According to Paul Valéry, a twentieth-century French poet and philosopher, "a fact poorly observed is more treacherous than faulty reasoning". Ian Mitroff in *Smart Thinking For Crazy Times* put it another way: many serious errors of management can be traced to solving the wrong problems precisely. If the team had undertaken some scenario planning in advance of plunging in, the unknown magnitude of the river's current would have been one of the key drivers in designing the scenarios. The other driver would have been the unknown combined physical stamina and co-ordination of the team under such circumstances. Using these two uncertainties as drivers, the unexpected outcome might have been captured in a scenario with a catchy name like "Deliverance". As Pierre Wack said: "It is better to be vaguely right than precisely wrong". Then you can make contingency plans – like walking back up the river to *that* tree, totally drenched to the bone!

It's all in the name

As we said earlier, graphic names for scenarios do help enormously in spreading the word. They become part of the in-house vernacular whenever the future is being discussed in a company. "Imperial Twilight" was one such name. It was applied to a scenario developed in the 1980s to show that the arms race between America and the Soviet Union was unsustainable because the Soviet Union was running out of money. The upshot would be the end of the Soviet Union, which is exactly what transpired. An environmental scenario sketched during the same decade was entitled "Rich Heritage". It drew attention to the fact that the present generation inhabiting the planet had to pass on to the next generation the same level of biodiversity as it had inherited. What one advertising executive said about brand names applies equally to scenario names. He commented: "A good name keeps the pie in the sky because pies on the ground are pretty boring objects." There's magic in a name!

At a recent workshop addressing job creation, a diverse body of interested parties identified the key uncertainties of job creation in the area as the commitment and involvement

of the communities within the area, and the level of investment from outside into the area. From this, four music-
themed scenarios were developed:

"PHILHARMONIC ORCHESTRA"

Potential investors, excited by the display of enthusiasm
and entrepreneurship of the community in the region, agree
to build a series of holiday resorts and develop factories
and commercial properties that will draw on the experience
and facilities in the region. This attracts more investment
and attention, resulting in a boost to tourism and the local
economy, providing jobs and opportunities for the community. The orchestra, made up of different clusters of skilled
instrumentalists, work together in harmony to produce a
world-class symphonic sound.

"CREATIVE DISCORD"

Excited by the arrival of potential investors, the local community put on a display of spontaneous enthusiasm and
entrepreneurship in the form of establishing a network of
separate markets. The investors, for whatever reason, decline to invest; but the community, now aware of their own
potential, maintain the momentum and the region becomes
a hotbed of entrepreneurial enterprises. The result: the communities play different tunes at different tempos. Although
the overall sound is discordant, each group of players is
bowled along by their own enthusiasm as they toot their
particular horns.

"LONELY BUSKER"

Investors, for whatever reason, decline to invest. The enthusiasm of the communities is low to nonexistent. Land issues are a major problem and no parties are willing to address the issues actively. Like the lonely busker on the street

pavement, playing his harmonica with his cap in his hand and hoping for the odd cent from a passer-by, each community survives by eking out a living.

Potential investors are excited about the area, see opportunities and plunge in. But there has been no prior consultation with the communities to examine what is best for the area. Each party has different expectations, with the consequence that investors stand over their subsequently abandoned factories and resorts like a conductor facing an empty orchestra pit.

Through the looking glass

When Alice protested through the looking glass that you can't believe impossible things, the Queen set the issue straight: "I daresay you haven't had much practice. When I was your age, I always did it for half an hour a day. Why, sometimes I've believed as many as six impossible things before breakfast." Lewis Carroll lit up the lives of many Victorian children by taking them into his world of make-believe. Coincidentally, in *Alice's Adventures in Wonderland*, hedgehogs feature as the balls in royal games of croquet with flamingoes as the mallets and soldiers – bent double – as the hoops. Since all three prefer to move of their own volition rather than behave as inert objects, the games usually end in chaos with the Queen calling for the heads of all those who misbehaved, and the king subsequently pardoning them.

The secret of successful scenario planning is not just the richness of the story line or the striking nature of the title. The content of the scenarios must also be relevant for them to come alive, not only in outer space, but also in inner space. Each person within a group has his or her own model of the real world and what is relevant based on his or her experiences. This is referred to as the person's "microcosm". The real world and its relevant parts are then the "macrocosm". Scenarios link the world of perception with the world of fact. In order to gain new insight from scenarios, one has to identify which information is of strategic importance and then transform it into material which penetrates the consciousness of the people for whom the information has potential consequences. It may not be new information but something that is already known and is right in front of the nose of the observers. It is just being misperceived. That is why Pierre Wack called scenario planning "the gentle art of reperceiving".

To put it in business terms: a company's *perception* of its business environment (microcosm) is as important as the actual state of the market (macrocosm) because its strategy comes from this perception. To be effective, then, the real target of scenario planning should be the microcosm of the decision makers. Unless their mental images of reality are influenced, the impact of scenarios will be negligible. In short: unless their minds are opened, their options will be closed. Pierre Wack cited the example of the oil scenarios he produced for Shell before the first oil price shock in the early 1970s. Although they were suitably prophetic in highlighting the instability of the market, they didn't connect with the senior executives of Shell. Pierre realised that unless he uncovered the managerial mind-set, his writing of further scenarios would be useless. He therefore did a whole series of interviews with managers to unearth what really made them tick and what language should be used to communicate new ideas to them. Consequently, Pierre's next set of scenarios on the second oil price shock, as we mentioned earlier on, really struck home.

It would be remiss of us as authors if we didn't end the scenario section with a golf story. After all, a round of golf has eighteen stories – one for each hole – and if you include the drink in the pub afterwards, nineteen. We have stressed on several occasions how scenario planning should embrace the unthinkable. Well, a photograph hanging in the corridor of the Durban Country Club reveals four golfers who played together and achieved just that. On the same par-four hole, the eighteenth, one player got an albatross, which is three under par and therefore a one; he drove the green. The second player got an eagle, which is two under par and therefore a two. The third and fourth players only managed a birdie and a par, in other words a three and a four. Now, would anyone in the entire golfing world ever write a scenario for that? It happened on 21 April 1994.

Options

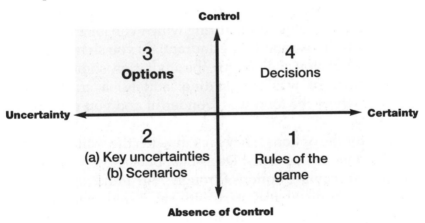

Food for thought

When Maggie Thatcher was British Prime Minister, she had a favourite phrase to overcome opposition in the Cabinet to any of her views – TINA, or there is no alternative. Hopefully, this section will demonstrate that TEMBA is a far better principle than TINA: there exist many better alternatives, all of which should be taken into consideration before you make the actual decision.

If you're the type of person who thinks we should cut to the chase and just make decisions, here's an example to prove that even you are susceptible to our type of matrix thinking. You have new neighbours who, to get acquainted, ask you out to a restaurant you've never been to before. The rules of the game for the evening are that you can only choose to eat what's on the menu of the selected restaurant and you have to be finished by closing time. The key uncertainties are whether the food and the service are good or bad at this unfamiliar restaurant, and whether your new neighbours are stimulating or dull. The scenarios flowing from these uncertainties are: (1) an evening where you doze off from tedium while wondering whether you have eaten something that was off; (2) a marvellous conversation with your neighbours during which you joke that next time you'll choose another restaurant; (3) you share little in common but you will return the invitation someday because the meal was outstanding; and (4) a crackerjack evening where the food was wonderful and you get along famously.

Now for the options. They kick in when the waiter brings you the menu. Decisions! Decisions! But before you make them, you play the options through your mind and across your taste buds. Shall I start with salad and then have a steak; or shall I go for soup and then have fish? When my neighbour asks me whether I like white or red wine, which shall I say? Am I going to finish with a sticky tart or cheese? Etc., etc. Yet, menus have many more applications today. Companies offer employees menus where for a certain monetary sum they will give you the chance of having a nice car but you then have to scrimp on the medical aid; or, vice versa, you can take lots of health insurance but then you drive around in a tin can. For hedgehogs who are used to being told exactly what their employment conditions are, the introduction of choice is bewildering. They are uncomfortable with options!

But it goes beyond restaurants and companies. Menus on what you can do on your computer; menus on aircraft offering a wide range of movies on your pop-up video screen; menus of occupations offered in career-guidance sessions; and, broader still, the astonishingly vast menus of consumer goods and services that well-off people nowadays face when they are choosing how to spend their disposable income – these all involve options. Indeed, technological progress is providing an infinite array of options. So you see, even if you're an action-oriented person, this section is for you.

Holidays in Chevrolets; jewellery and rugby

"Are we there yet?" We have all asked the question as youngsters on a long car journey to a holiday destination. The only oases of relief were the stops to refuel along the way. Imagine a child who has seemingly endured this lifetime on the back seat persistently nagging his family that at the next stop he be allowed into the refreshment area to buy *one* item for the next leg of the journey. The family acquiesces to shut him up. As he excitedly enters the store, he is confronted by a veritable cornucopia of sweets, popcorn, potato chips and cold drinks. Shelves upon shelves of wonderful mouth-watering goodies and he is allowed to pick anything – as long as it's one thing and he doesn't make a mess in the car! Does he have a seemingly unlimited range of options? No. He has a tremendous range of *opportunities* but his *options* are limited. The difference? Opportunities only become options when they *fall within your control*.

One of the beauties of scenario planning is that it provides real choices for action. These choices are not random possibilities but are specifically relevant to our situation because they have been developed out of the earlier processes identified in our matrix. The richer the scenarios, the more varied the options. What makes options particularly important is that although they are derived from uncertainties outside our control, they are restricted to actions within our control. As such, the third quadrant is enthusiastically explored by foxes but is somewhat of a no-go area for hedgehogs. Whereas hedgehogs are dead-set on following a chosen path, foxes are guided by instinct. Consequently, whenever the path ahead forks and involves a choice, foxes are quite ready to venture off the straight and narrow to explore alternatives that are "beyond reason". In that sense, the left-hand side of our matrix represents the (more intuitive) right-hand side of our brain.

Control is power. But the true nature of power is having control in times of uncertainty. That control comes in the form of options; so the person who can exercise more options in the face of uncertainty has more power. Pierre Wack once wrote two scenarios for the world of gold – "Plan" or "Be Planned". His point was simple. Either gold-mining companies roll up their sleeves and get involved in the downstream retail market of jewellery and thereby influence demand; or they should expect to bob up and down in the ripples to the gold price caused by central bank sales. He maintained that the power of oil companies lay in the fact that they have so many options to play around with between the well in the ground and the filling station in the village. Vertical integration has its advantages – it turns you into a price-maker as opposed to a price-taker. This wasn't bad advice, since a feature of mining is how long it takes to sink a shaft and come into production. All that money flowing out and the only relevant price is the one you get when you're up and running! It makes sense to influence it, particularly with gold being the oldest brand around – signifying sun, sex, power, money and winning the race. What more do you want?

Now it's time for us to give you our own tip. Keep your eyes on the rules of the game: if they change, then the options can change too. For example, until recently, the rules of rugby stated that if a side was awarded a penalty and they decided to kick the ball into touch, the throw-in was then awarded to the opposing team. This meant transferring control of the game to the opposition. When this rule was changed so that the team awarded the penalty could kick the ball into touch and still have the throw-in, it provided an exciting new option. If a team is now given a penalty close to the opposing try line, they can kick for the posts for three points; or go for touch *closer* to the tryline in the knowledge that if they score a try and convert it, they will obtain an extra seven points. The implication of this rule amendment is that rugby becomes a much more interesting game to watch when the score is close in the dying minutes of a match. Business has the same fascination for a different reason: the rules are changing all the time, creating new windows of opportunity and new options.

Stars and dogs and Apollo 13 continued

A way of getting managers to discuss strategic options is illustrated in the diagram overleaf. If a company wants to assess the value of its underlying businesses, ask the board to post each business into the appropriate square. Is it a core star, a noncore star, a core dog or a noncore dog? We all know what to do with core stars – keep them. Equally, we

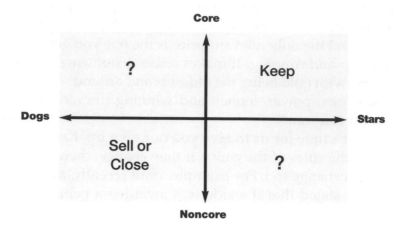

know what to do with noncore dogs – get rid of them or, as they say in the veterinary profession, put them down. But what do you do with noncore stars and core dogs? You might wish to hang on to the former because they consistently contribute to your financial results. On the other hand, with focus being in fashion, you might decide to sell them for a decent sum and use the money to invest more into your core businesses.

Core dogs are different. So much management time is spent trying to turn a core dog around that, after the 51st restructuring, everybody is sick to death of it. Basically, you can re-engineer a dog as much as you like and it still barks! So as Jack Welch, Chairman of General Electric, puts it: the options are fix, sell or close. Then, just to make matters complicated, the rules of the game can change, turning a dog into a star (a dog-star!) or a star into a dog.

Speaking of stars, let's not forget about the three astronauts still hanging in on board Apollo 13. The three scenarios of possible outcomes described earlier – "Close but No Cigar", "Tin Tomb" and "Sweet as Apple Pie" – would have provided the astronauts and the support team in Mission Control with the most realistic options available. The objective was obviously to bring the astronauts home alive. However there was no instruction manual for what should be done under such circumstances. In this unique life-threatening situation, therefore, the range and detail of the scenarios were essential in order to develop as many options as possible to help them make the most effective ongoing decisions. So what options within their control would they have had? Among them were to:

– conserve power by shutting down all but the critical systems;

– conserve water by rationing;

– reduce carbon dioxide levels by attempting to adapt the filtering system in the lunar module;

– use the sun as a navigational point of reference, debris around the lunar module having made it virtually impossible to see the stars;

– try and increase speed around the moon to give them enough momentum to sling them onto a path back to Earth;

– try and redirect power to critical systems; and

– exercise a "burn", which would use power, to correct their path at the right moment.

Although, in retrospect, the options for the crew of the Apollo 13 may have seemed logical and orderly, the crew's method of implementation certainly wasn't. This is an essential point to bear in mind: options are only effective if they can be implemented; otherwise they're just "good ideas". Time was not on the side of the crew and Mission Control, so the implementation depended on close teamwork. For example, a whole new flight plan was needed to put the astronauts on a fresh course for home. This would normally have required three months. Mission Control managed it in three days. The exact time and duration of a "burn" to change their alignment so that the orbit around the moon would slingshot the spacecraft back towards the Earth had to be calculated. This was one of those rare moments that maths teachers will forever boast about, as it showed the importance of a healthy knowledge of vector calculus! The problem of connecting the square lithium hydroxide canisters of the command module to the round openings of the lunar module environmental system to remove carbon dioxide build-up required creative thought on the part of engineers on Earth. They had to do a dummy run with materials similar to those that were available on board the craft. This was achieved using piping, plastic bags and cardboard, all connected and sealed with tape.

Interestingly, the same tape that was used to save the lives of the crew may well have been the product of a truly foxy company, which presents a good example of flexibility and adaptability. It is forever developing new options in the face of a changing market environment. 3M, whose name is synonymous with Scotch Tape, started as Minnesota Mining and Manufacturing. As times and circumstances changed, they evolved into a sandpaper manufacturer; then into adhesive tape invented by a banjo-playing engineer; Post-it notes; and more recently high-tech optics. Here is a company that is in control of its destiny and has exploited uncertainty to its advantage. It has thrived by retaining its greatest strength through thick and thin – innovation.

To summarise, realistic and action-oriented strategic planning requires options. Formulate as many options as possible and then look realistically at those that are achievable and can most effectively be implemented by you. Remember that options aren't recommendations, just as scenarios aren't forecasts. So be as "blue sky" as you like in a discussion on options. If people think your option is too wild, you can always say it was just an option. Whereas one option, or even part of one, is used in the end, you can only confidently proceed if all the alternatives have been identified and rejected. In this way, options give you more control and allow you the comfort and certainty that you made the best decision you could under the circumstances – even if you are subsequently proved wrong.

Returning to golf, the options are the clubs in your bag. Each club is there to strike the ball a different distance. It is only when you're out there on the course that you'll decide which club to use, depending on your distance from the hole, your lie and the wind. Making decisions without considering the options is rather like playing a golf course with only one club in your bag – difficult.

Decisions

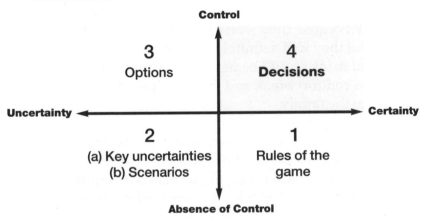

Chocolates, white water rafting and a world cup final

Remember our young friend at the beginning of the last section who is about to step into a child's dream and a dentist's nightmare? He is allowed any item in the shop providing it's one thing and won't make a mess. Those are the rules! So he has opportunities. However, if he is clever, he will realise that there are several uncertainties influencing his choice. He is aware that there is still quite a journey ahead but he is uncertain how long it will be before the next stop. Moreover, he is uncertain whether or not he will be allowed a similar treat at the next stop. So, does he look for something that will last, or go for quick gratification, assuming he can get something at the next stop? You can imagine the options that will plague his young mind:

– a packet of sweets. They will last, but then he runs the risk of the rest of the family piling into the packet;

– a chocolate bar. It will have to be eaten quickly if it's hot in the car. But the chances are that if he grudgingly thrusts a gooey piece towards his family, they'll hastily refuse his offer. So he'll eat the whole thing himself with the downside that it could make him thirsty;

– potato chips or popcorn. They are a good idea if it's a long way because they won't melt. But they could still get messy and they will definitely make him thirsty.

– a cold drink would be nice. But he might have to ask to stop for a comfort break and that won't go down well with the rest of the family.

So now, out of that heavenly expanse of tasty opportunities which define his options, how will he make the best decision? The answer, according to our matrix, is entirely in his hands; but at least it will be an informed decision. Forrest Gump had a perceptive mother whose simple and somewhat idealistic philosophy was that life is like a box of chocolates – a tempting array of options ready for the picking and any decision is rewarded with anything but a bitter taste in the mouth. That's Hollywood for you! The reality, of course, is that in business and in life, the challenges and opportunities offered are seldom like those neatly displayed before the kid in the candy store. They are more like those encountered by our intrepid team of rafters out for a bit of bonding on the river and who, after *not* working through our matrix, are now huddled together and hurtling down a raging torrent. It matters not that they are down the creek with paddles as opposed to up the creek without them. They still have to make an effective decision.

The present trend in global markets is like a swelling current. Panic is starting to set in down corporate corridors as it becomes obvious that ahead lies a more volatile global economy with the possibility of a very bumpy ride. We are now white water rafting! Anyone who has wilfully engaged in this struggle with Mother Nature will bear testimony to how thrilling it can be. But it invariably claims some victims. This is where teamwork and decisions will either thrill you or kill you. Abandoning control and jumping off the raft is dangerous, and so is losing control, hitting a rock and falling off. The best decisions in this particular situation will come from working through the matrix – identifying the rules of the game, establishing the key uncertainties, constructing scenarios and drawing up the options available. That way you make decisions which mean that you squeeze between the rocks and make it to the calmer waters further downstream.

If you don't mind, we'd like to put you in a very uncomfortable situation. Imagine the scene: it's the Soccer World Cup Final. At the final whistle both teams are tied 1-1, and extra time yields no further goals. The match goes to a penalty shoot-out, five penalties each. Team A have scored five penalties and Team B have scored four with one penalty left. Congratulations – you are the goalkeeper for Team A facing the last penalty. If you save it, your team wins 5-4 on penalties; and the most coveted trophy in the world of sport is yours, together with instant fame and millions of dollars in endorsements. If the ball gets past you, it's a sudden-death penalty play-off, and the game continues. Pressure. Lots of it. Do you dive to the left or to the right? No self-respecting goalie would walk on the field at this level without having played this scenario over and over in his mind. He would have factored into his matrix the likely line-up of penalty-takers on the other side; whether they are left- or right-footed; whether they favour kicking the ball to the left or right; and whether they favour kicking it high or low. By running through this information on the last player who is about to shoot, you, as the goalie, will be as prepared as you can be. Whether or not you eventually make the right decision is not the issue. You did your best – and this is how the true stars of sport are born.

A successful failure

Let's return to the story that we've made a focal point of this book – the crew of the Apollo 13. It's decision time, and the decisions of our three foxes in space are now emblazoned in the history books. Firstly, the crew moved into the lunar module and shut down the power to all but the non-critical systems. This decision took into account the drop in temperature that would be caused by a loss in power. They had played the scenario that the resultant build-up of moisture through condensation could pose the danger of arcing when the power-up to jettison the lunar module was required for splashdown. They decided to take this risk on the grounds that any arcing would be controlled by safeguards built into the command module after the disastrous fire aboard Apollo 1 in January 1967.

The second decision was to conserve water, as it was no longer being produced after the oxygen tank explosion. This decision was made when it was realised that, at the ordinary rate of consumption, their water supply would be exhausted five hours before the essential water-cooling required for Earth re-entry. However, the data from the Apollo 11 flight showed that the craft's mechanisms could survive seven to eight hours in space without water-cooling. Again this decision was based on a previous experience and therefore was backed by a degree of certainty. The third decision related to the use of whatever materials were available to connect the square lithium hydroxide canisters, used for removing carbon dioxide from the command module, to the round openings in the lunar module. This was a classic case of implementing a decision based on the resources available.

The fourth decision was to remain on a moon trajectory instead of using valuable power to turn the craft around and head back to Earth. They would then use the gravitational pull of the moon to slingshot the craft back on a course for home. This decision was made with the knowledge that to stop the craft, turn it around and power it back would use up all its power. Given the orbital dynamics of the moon, a small burn would do. They had worked through the options!

The final two decisions were the really tricky ones. They had to utilise two burns at exactly the right time and angle in order to speed up the craft on the route home and effect the survival of the crew. This decision could only be made with precise measurements of speed, trajectory and direction. The first of the two burns on the route back from the moon's orbit was the most critical in that it required absolute certainty of the position of the craft in relation to the Earth. It also involved a rotation of the craft that would enable the astronauts to use the sun as the most accurate point of alignment for the rest of the trip. When the craft was rotated to the attitude Houston had requested, the sun was where it was expected to be – in fact it proved to be less than half a degree off. The decision to rotate at that moment was instrumental in bringing the crew home. In the book *Apollo Expeditions to the Moon*, the words of the Flight Director Gerald Griffin convey the tension and excitement leading up to the final burn which shortened the time home: "Some years later when I went back to the log and looked up that mission, my writing was almost illegible I was so damned nervous. And I remember the exhilaration running through me. My God, that's kind of the last hurdle. If we can do that I know we can make it. It was funny because only the people involved knew how important it was to have that platform properly aligned."

What is noteworthy is that no decision was made in and of itself. The success of the adjusted mission to bring the astronauts safely back to Earth was the result of many decisions shaped by incremental actions and the information they produced. Overall the experiences gathered throughout the whole mission contributed to a better understanding of a variety of factors, including the dynamics and dangers of space flight; possible rescue procedures; decisions that might be made in preparation for future missions; and the benefits of good teamwork under extraordinary circumstances. This, and the fact that the crew managed to return safely, prompted Commander Jim Lovell to call the mission a "successful failure".

Let's put this experience into a business context. It can be argued that the most successful companies are those that are best at learning, having discovered that effective decision-making is essentially a learning process involving experimentation and teamwork. This is in line with the "personal construct" theory as put forward by its main proponent, George Kelley. He believed that we make decisions based on our own constructs, which in turn are derived from our experiences, our previous decisions and what we have learnt from them. This theory therefore highlights the fact that our decisions are limited if we cut ourselves off from the experiences and opinions of others. To varying degrees, such decisions turn out to be self-centred and narrow in scope – typical of the reclusive hedgehog. What scenario planning encourages is the expanding of our constructs through dialogue with others around a broader range of possibilities – the typical pattern of sociable foxes. This opens the way for decisions which are unthinkable when considered in isolation. Symbiosis was an essential ingredient in the production of this book. Neither of us could have done it on our own. You build on each other's ideas.

A question that is often asked when we present the matrix at workshops is: "It sounds like a lengthy process; do you have to work through the entire matrix before making every decision?" The answer is that first time round you should. Subsequently, the matrix need only be updated when circumstances change. The important thing to remember is that, because the matrix represents a natural thought process, reference to it is ongoing. Whether we are making the decision to go for the fish or the beef offered by a stewardess on board a domestic flight; or whether we are about to agree to a multi-billion dollar merger with another company, we may return to the matrix more than once. We've all had second thoughts!

Unless something arrives like a bolt out of the blue and requires a split second decision – even then the matrix is implicitly used – the lead-up to a decision should involve the continual feeding of information into the matrix and upgrading or changing that information as the situation develops. For example, had our involuntary white water rafters prepared for being swept downstream, they might have worked out whether to go left or right of the first rock they encountered. Once committed to a decision, they would wait for the outcome before adjusting their options for the next challenge. At least, by returning to the matrix again and again, they would give themselves the opportunity to refine their decisions as they progressed down the rapids. Moreover, even if the outcome of a decision were not the intended or expected one, experience and information would *still* be gained and fed into the matrix for the next decision. As we've already said on several occasions, decisions and actual outcomes may be far apart. Tracking the convergence or divergence between result and intention is as important as going through the matrix in the first place. It tells you how much you have to adjust your original plan. Napoleon once remarked that "the problem is always in the execution, not the idea".

Go, fly a kite

Feedback loops like the one we've just described are central to the process of scientific thought. They have been the intellectual driving force behind some of the most important discoveries in the history of mankind. Hypotheses are established which result in experiments being done. The outcomes modify the hypothesis, leading to the conduct of further experiments and so on. Armed with an ever-increasing body of data and an ever-decreasing gap between hypothesis and fact, scientists eventually put forward their hypotheses as scientific propositions subject to peer review. If they pass muster, over time they become law. But that is not the end of it. Later generations may modify the law if it breaks down under certain circumstances. The law is obsolete rather than untrue. We still use classical physics in our everyday world of objects because it is perfectly satisfactory. However, in the realm of the quantum and the quark, the laws have changed. Science should be seen as a body of knowledge which is grown incrementally by each generation of scientists. Aristotle, Newton, Einstein – they inherited the genius of all who came before and left behind their own indelible footprints.

Sometimes you're lucky. Benjamin Franklin, the eighteenth-century printer, author, philosopher, diplomat, scientist and one of the founding fathers of American "foxology", proved his hypothesis that lightning was an electrical charge without requiring a feedback loop. He flew a kite during an electrical storm in 1752. Attached, as the popular story goes, to the wet string was a key. Before he made the decision to fly the kite, he had worked through the matrix and in particular the scientific rules of the game. He estimated that, given the electrical nature of lightning, a charge should manifest itself in the key if the kite was struck. At the same time, he had an almost fatal ignorance of the intensity of the charge released by a bolt of lightning. Lightning did strike the kite, the key was charged and the rest, as they say, is history. Fortunately, he survived the experiment and went on to invent, amongst many other things, the lightning rod, bifocal spectacles and the Franklin stove. He also offered the "one-fluid" theory which distinguished between positive and negative electricity. In recognition of all his scientific accomplishments he received honorary degrees from the University of St Andrews and Oxford University.

For most people entry to such eminent universities is through hard work, dedication, lots of studying and more hard work. But is the enthusiastic embracing of this kind of academia the best decision for young people leaving school? In his "biography" of the world's most famous equation, $E=mc^2$, David Bodanis recounts Albert Einstein's sister, Maja, telling of the now infamous event in her brother's schooling when his Greek teacher complained to her that nothing would ever come of Albert Einstein. She adds: "And in fact Albert Einstein never did attain a professorship of Greek grammar." Indeed, it was as a humble in-spector of patents in Bern that he broke upon the world scene with his special theory of relativity. Presumably, he was rebuilding the universe in his head while he was sort-ing through the patent documents.

The new generation of nineteen-year-old entrepreneurs in the information technology field are not your average school-leavers. They are uninhibited enough to think noth-ing of breaking new ground. They are quite at ease on the left-hand side of the matrix, handling the uncertainties of new start-ups and dreaming up amazing options to push technology to its limits. Diplomas and degrees are not their measure of success. For them, success comes from taking the foxier route associated with true entrepreneurial spirit. Many have made their millions that way. The secret is a "can do" outlook. This comes from an awareness of what they can control and what they can't; and then from experi-menting with different options in mapping out their future until they find the right one. This is why we should encour-age our children to be familiar with and work through the matrix. It will give them the ability to make genuine assess-ments of the manifold pathways opening up before them rather than relying on guesswork. A wonderful piece of Irish wisdom goes like this: "If you don't know where you're going, any road will take you there." At the very least, we should give our kids a guidance system!

One of the problems of the normal school curriculum is that it is firmly planted on the right-hand side of our matrix. As a pupil, you learn to respect the rules of the game – be it the rules of the school, the rules of English grammar or the rules of arithmetic; but you don't learn to identify key un-certainties, sketch scenarios and choose between options. You don't learn how to handle the world of grey where de-cisions are anything but clear-cut. Parents think that it's supportive to say to a child "'be what you want to be". In reality, we should be saying to our children the more assertive "be what you can be and don't miss out". Fly the kite! By developing self-confidence and the faculty of curiosity in our children, we are equipping them with the most powerful tool for shaping their future and to give them the edge – the Mind of a Fox. When people ask you what do you do in future, remember the foxy answer is: "I do what I can."

The matrix in action

Having gone through the four quadrants of the matrix in some detail, we now want to demonstrate how it works in practice as a whole. What better way to kick off this process than a letter from the authors to the White House offering some friendly advice on the future to the new incumbent.

Dear Mr President,

Congratulations on attaining the most powerful position in the world. However, like all other jobs, there are constraints on what you can do. We're not talking of the checks and balances written into the US Constitution limiting your power vis-à-vis Congress and the Supreme Court. We want to list some rules of the game for the world – rules which are pretty certain to operate during your presidency and which are beyond your control.

Let's start with the demographics. Basically, the world is divided into two camps. There are the "rich old millions" – some 900 million to be more precise – who live in the developed world. We call them old because their birth rate has been declining, longevity has been increasing and a geriatric boom is underway. Immigrants, though, from the developing world provide a significant infusion of youth. This latter world consists of just over five billion people of whom nearly half reside in China and India. We classify them as the "poor young billions". Obviously, the split is not quite as simple as this as there are poor people in rich countries and rich people in poor countries. Nevertheless, for our purposes, this picture accurately serves as the first rule of the game. While you won't be able to change this picture much even if you serve two presidential terms, you can set in motion a process that begins to eradicate poverty quite significantly – probably the number one objective in the minds of most people with a conscience in the world today.

This, however, leads to the second rule of the game – globalisation. We now have more open markets than probably at any previous time in our history, but equally we have greater economic competition between nations. Competition implies winners and losers. The world economy is not exactly a zero-sum game, because among the poor young billions have been some winners, notably Asian Tigers like South Korea and Taiwan and parts of China, India and South America. And among the losers are some countries which are there, not because they've been driven to the wall by competition, but because they're miserably governed. Even so, it is not unsurprising that the main result of globalisation so far has been to confer the most benefits upon those who were the favourites in the first place. As they say, to the victors go the spoils and you were already a victor before anybody else had time to get out of the starting blocks. In fact, America has done so well out of globalisation that it is fast becoming a one-horse race – Europe and Japan having dropped behind in the economic race and Russia in the arms race.

We don't want to be party-poopers and spoil your celebrations, particularly with talk now of a "hard landing" in your economy; but we have an untenable state of affairs in light of the third rule of the game. We are one world and too many losers will ultimately bring you down along with everybody else. For good or ill, we are becoming more interdependent, which means each of us has less control over our own destiny. Think of what would happen if the oil stopped flowing from the Middle East!

Unlike the 100-metre dash where nobody's performance is affected by anybody else's on the track, the world economy has to grow for America to continue growing. Your multinational companies and exports like Hollywood movies both increasingly rely on prosperous markets outside America. For America's foreign customers to be prosperous, they also have to produce and sell their goods and services at a profit to you and each other. While some (the rich) are doing this, the majority (the poor) aren't, and now labour under the load of an international debt that they cannot repay. While you have a full-employment economy and can boast about it, most developing economies have a serious unemployment problem. They have no means of getting out of the quagmire as long as a significant amount of their budget goes towards repaying debt, and your world-class companies can outsmart and outmanoeuvre any fledgling industries they try to nurture. In short, we are a seriously dysfunctional global family with you at the head and the younger children in hock.

But being one family in one world, we have a new rule of the game that has crept up upon us over the last fifty years – global climate change. We have selected this phrase rather than global warming because there remains some uncertainty among the scientists as to the degree of warming that is taking place. The one thing that cannot be denied, however, is a rise in the frequency and scale of extreme events like droughts, floods, hailstorms and hurricanes as the global climate moves through a series of temporary states to a new equilibrium. These events also affect more people, given that the world population has doubled since 1962. If the evidence grows that the world is indeed warming up significantly and this can be linked to carbon emissions, guess who has to make the biggest sacrifice in bringing down fossil fuel consumption? – America! You have to lead the way instead of shifting the burden of change elsewhere. In this regard, your evident hostility to the Kyoto protocol on global warming was not exactly helpful. Perhaps, in a few hundred years, people will look back at our energy profligacy with the same sense of disbelief that we entertain for our ancestors' attitude to slavery.

Yet another consequence of being one family multiplying on one Earth is the growing possibility of worldwide epidemics. We already have the phenomenon of HIV/AIDS. Although it appears to be no longer a threat to the rich old millions, it is still spreading among the poor young billions. You cannot have healthy economies with sick people: thus HIV/AIDS may stymie efforts to help the poor nations to catch up the rich. But don't relax. With urbanisation, migration and the mutation of bacteria and viruses into drug-resistant forms, an old-fashioned plague of some kind which will affect everyone is looming large; and the doctors' arsenal of antibiotics is looking desperately thin. It may be the animals the rich eat which do them in. Or it may be something as simple as a new strain of the good old staphylococcus aureus microbe which up till now has been held in check by penicillin.

We would like to complete the rules to which you are subject on a positive note. The rapid spread of products spawned by the latest technological wave – cellphones, personal computers, the Internet and genetically engineered

	Control	
3 **Options** *Constructive engagement* *Isolation*		**4** **Decisions** ?
Uncertainty ←		→ **Certainty**

2
(a) Key uncertainties
Nuclear terrorism
Disintegration of world
  order
(b) Scenarios
Friendly Planet
Gilded Cage
		1
		Rules of the game
		Demographics
		Globalisation
		Global climate change
		Potential for epidemics
		New technological wave
		Favourable values for
		  economic growth

	Absence of Control	

crops and medicines – has produced an unprecedented period of economic growth for some. Talk is of the "new economy" and the "long boom" if we can get through the current downturn. The challenge is to make these advances even more pervasive in the developing world and allow them to leapfrog over previous generations of technology. Adding further momentum to the process is the fact that values supportive of business and free enterprise have become more widespread. Governments are moving towards a pragmatic blend of ideologies: they are taking a pinch of this-ism and a pinch of that-ism, putting them into a pot and concocting a brew that works for them.

But what of possible surprises beyond your control? We call them key uncertainties. From your point of view, nuclear weapons landing up in the wrong hands must be at the top of the agenda. Proliferation means aggravation, and the knowledge of how to construct a nuclear device is now freely available on the Internet. So it's just a matter of time before somebody really nasty gathers the money, the materials and the engineering skills necessary to manufacture it.

119

You only need one terrorist organisation to hold the rich old millions to ransom by planting a hidden nuclear bomb in the middle of one city for everyone to realise that conventional military capability is useless against such a threat. An army can't find a needle in a haystack, let alone destroy it. Or it could be a rogue state which in secret develops nuclear-tipped rockets with sufficient range to reach a Western city. Incidentally, we haven't even mentioned the threat of the poor man's "nuke" – biological and chemical weapons.

The other key uncertainty that we'd worry about – if we were you – is a general disintegration of world order caused by age-old motivations of greed, power and ethnic and religious hatred. The interventions that you've recently made to keep the peace in trouble spots around the world like Somalia and the Gulf have been costly; and, increasingly, parents don't want their sons to risk their lives and health on problems which have nothing to do with the United States. The hazards associated with exposure to depleted uranium have made the Europeans equally unenthusiastic. And the United Nations has neither the money nor the clout to take on the role of global cop.

So what are the scenarios that arise from these rules of the game and key uncertainties? We'll sketch two mainframe scenarios which for convenience are named "Friendly Planet" and "Gilded Cage". In Friendly Planet the rich old millions resolve to find common ground with the poor young billions to eradicate poverty and disease, to tackle problems of the environment, to bring international criminal syndicates to justice and to root out dangerous terrorist organisations. All nations jointly agree to solve any problems which are a threat to world peace. It sounds terribly utopian, but the alternative for the rich old millions is to hole themselves up in a Gilded Cage. That cage could be blown to smithereens at any moment by nuclear-armed terrorists or be gradually overwhelmed by millions of illegal immigrants slipping through the bars to escape anarchy elsewhere. The law of entropy will prevail as nations descend to a common low.

Now we come to the options inside your control as leader of the most powerful nation in the free world. You can either turn outwards and engage in a process of constructive dialogue with a representative sample of leaders from the developing world. This leads to a set of concrete action programmes by the rich old millions which do not involve hand-outs but the empowerment of poor people to help themselves. The emphasis is on small community initiatives which induce self-sufficiency and create small circles of responsibility and accountability, rather than grand, majestic projects which increase dependency and line a few pockets. The rich also level the playing field by getting rid of their tariffs and quotas on foodstuffs and other goods imported from the developing world. Even though the US has the power to do as it pleases – remember the story of the big gorilla sleeping where he wants to – enlightened self-interest dictates that the gorilla can't have it both ways on globalisation. We don't know whether you play golf but it's like the richest members of the club giving themselves a handicap but denying everyone else in the club the right to do so. Not only is it unfair, it is counterproductive to the health and spirit of the club.

The alternative and less favourable option is that you turn inwards and try to isolate yourself from the poor young billions by making the cage you live in impenetrable to outsiders unless they are highly skilled, in which case you allow them through the bars. We know that you belong to a party which has a tendency to go this route. But human ingenuity being what it is and necessity being the mother of invention, desperately poor people will always find ways of breaching your barricades. Furthermore, the reciprocal of an isolationist strategy is that Americans will become less and less welcome in the developing world as widespread resentment over the negative impacts of globalisation turns into fury. There are plenty of social activists already fanning the flames. American tourists are notoriously twitchy about security and will therefore increasingly confine themselves to home base. There's no fun in being taken hostage while on holiday.

If you want to make a big footprint on this Earth and go down as one of the great presidents of the first century of the new millennium, think about the first option. Like the great social reformers of the late nineteenth century re-shaped industrialisation to give it a more human face, you have the chance of reshaping globalisation so that it brings more benefits to the poor young billions. It's your call, Mr President.

Yours sincerely,
Two South African Foxes.

High Road or Low Road?

We now turn to an actual scenario exercise that dates back to the mid-1980s. It concerned the possible political and economic paths that South Africa might take into the 1990s. The principal architects of the study were Michael O'Dowd and Bobby Godsell, two Anglo American employees, who in turn based their model on some original work done by a French political risk analyst, Edouard Parker.

The foremost rule of the game governing South Africa's future at the time was a simple one. Because the whites had the guns and the blacks had the numbers, no "winner-takes-all" scenario existed. If the whites hung on to power, there'd be a rising tide of violence which would be unstoppable. If the blacks tried to take the country by force, they'd fail or,

Control

3
Options
Political – winner-takes-all
versus compromise
Economic – status quo
versus transformation

4
Decisions
Political – the High Road
Economic – ?

Uncer-tainty

Certainty

2
(a) Key uncertainties
Strategies of power
Economic strategies
World/SA dynamic
(b) Scenarios
High Road
Low Road

1
Rules of the game
No winner-takes-all outcome
Interim need for power-sharing
Economic realities eroding
 apartheid
Negotiation transforms individuals
Conditions for a winning nation
 equally apply to South Africa

Absence of Control

after a long struggle, inherit a wasteland. A second rule therefore followed from the first: a positive scenario could only materialise for the country if there was compromise on both sides and some interim formula for sharing power was agreed. Thereafter South Africa could, and should, evolve into a genuine, representative democracy.

The third rule related to South Africa being a modern industrialised society with comparative advantages like abundant mineral resources, cheapish power, an important trade route around its coast, beautiful tourist spots and proximity to African markets. These economic realities had already nudged companies and trade unions into power-sharing arrangements, and were undermining the last remnants of statutory apartheid. Moreover, the daily contact at work between people of all backgrounds, and the imperative of getting on with the job, pre-empted a French or Russian-type revolution. So the signs were good.

The fourth rule was an interesting psychological one. If only one could get all the parties around the negotiating table and throw away the key to the room, it would transform their attitudes. Personal chemistry and familiarity would make each side see the individuals on the other side of the table for what they really were – not devils with horns and tails but pretty ordinary people with virtues and vices like everybody else.

The fifth and last rule was drawn from the global scenario study that was being conducted in parallel to the South African one. It concerned the portrait of a "winning nation". For any nation to win in the sense of achieving a sustained growth in income per head, six conditions needed to be fulfilled: (1) a high standard of education; (2) a strong work ethic which in turn rested on small, non-intrusive government, a sound family system, low taxation and minimal corruption; (3) mobilisation of capital to satisfy the needs of the new generation of entrepreneurs; (4) a dual-logic economy in which there were positive synergies between large world-class mining, manufacturing and service industries on one hand and the small business and informal sector on the other; (5) social harmony in which minorities co-existed happily with the majority; and (6) an ambition to look outwards and be a global player. These six attributes were as applicable to South Africa as to any other nation on Earth if it wanted to succeed economically.

Against this background, three key uncertainties were identified. The first revolved around the strategies of power that might be adopted by the contending parties at the time. Would they go for winner-takes-all or would they negotiate in a spirit of give-and-take? If either side went for winner-takes-all, the other side would be compelled to follow suit. The second uncertainty related to economic strategies. Would whoever ruled in the future adopt the kind of pragmatic policies necessary to turn South Africa into a winning nation or would they go for a heavy-handed, ideological ap-

124

proach? The third uncertainty was the future dynamic between the world and South Africa. Would sanctions remain or would they be dropped and South Africa be welcomed back into the fold?

This produced two principal scenarios. The first was the "High Road" of negotiation leading to political settlement. This had to be followed shortly thereafter by the implementation of economic strategies which would propel South Africa to winning nation status. The "Low Road" was a story of confrontation leading to conflict and eventually a civil war which would reduce South Africa to rubble. Simple choice. Most experts at the time expected South Africa to take the Low Road because no government had ever negotiated itself out of power. In retrospect and against all odds, South Africa took the political High Road because there were outstanding individuals on all sides who put the country ahead of their personal and their party's interests. A government of national unity acted as a precursor to a fully fledged democracy. The events were amazing and unthinkable, but they illustrated the power of scenario planning, because nobody was brave enough at the time to *forecast* what actually happened. Instead, a possibility became a probability and a probability became a reality.

However, the second crossroads – the economic one – is still ahead for South Africa. Political transformation has yet to be followed by economic transformation and the common vision to give a better life to all has yet to be implemented. The foxes, namely all those young entrepreneurs who dream of starting their own businesses, are still out in the cold. This leads us to the two rules of the economic game which have to be obeyed in order to create a winning economy. The first is money times velocity (the number of hands it passes through in a year) equals price times transactions. This equation tells you two things: (1) if you just

125

pump money into the economy without increasing economic activity (transactions), all that happens is that prices rise and inflation takes off; but (2) if you really want to light the candle of economic growth, you have to increase the velocity of circulation of money, which means pushing up the number of transactions. How do you achieve the latter? The answer is to promote the dual-logic economy referred to earlier as the fourth characteristic of a winning nation. This will involve a dynamic link between small, entrepreneurially run businesses and the existing world-class multinationals in South Africa: they buy and sell from each other as well as export overseas. The second economic rule is savings equals investment: if people don't save, you won't have capital to invest and therefore satisfy the third condition of a winning nation – mobilisation of capital. To get the public to save, you can't just *tell* them to do so. Rather you have to *induce* them through tax concessions on interest received or by offering higher interest rates on small deposits. In short, the finance minister has to be foxy too and realise that money is like manure: it's better when it's spread around a bit! And if it isn't, Karl's rule comes into play – as in Marx: when the mass of the population feel they have zero prospects, expect a revolution.

As a footnote, HIV/AIDS was picked up on the Anglo scenario team's radar screen in the mid-1980s. In those days it was described as a wild card – something that might affect South Africa's future, but nobody knew how and to what extent. Now the epidemic has been elevated to a rule of the game because it is impossible to eradicate under any scenario in the short term. The next section deals with it in more detail.

The Second Struggle

The sexual rules of the game have changed since 1965 when unsafe sex was defined as "not remembering to put the Mini's handbrake on" or "two drive-ins in a weekend". Now it is a matter of life and death. With the fall of apartheid, South Africa faces a second struggle against an enemy more formidable than any human foe because of its stealth and invisibility – HIV / AIDS.

The first two rules of the game are simple: HIV causes AIDS and, unlike other diseases, kills mainly young people who are in the prime of their life. The third rule is the lethal one in the long run. The virus has a delayed action. If it killed people immediatly like the Ebola virus, preventive actions to halt its spread would be taken by society and individuals

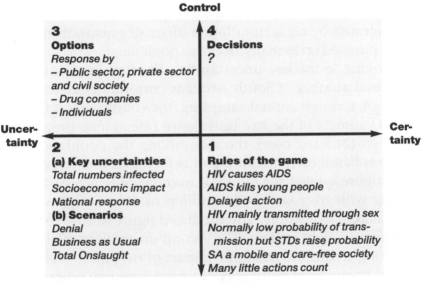

alike. As it is, denial is possible until it is too late. The fourth rule is that in South Africa the virus is mainly transmitted through unsafe sex: in other countries the chief culprit is drug injection. The fifth rule is that, under normal conditions, HIV has quite a low probability of transmission. However, the sixth rule is that South Africa has a high frequency of untreated sexually transmitted diseases (STDs) like syphilis and gonorrhea; and if either sexual partner or both have an STD, the chances of transmission rise dramatically. The seventh rule is that South Africa is a mobile society with a fairly carefree attitude towards activities like drinking, driving and sex. The combination of people having multiple sexual partners dispersed over a wide geographic area with low or no use of condoms offers an ideal environment for the virus to spread. The eighth and last rule is that there is no magic bullet to turn the epidemic around. It will be defeated by an accumulation of small grassroots initiatives pursued on as many fronts as possible.

Moving to the key uncertainties, the first one concerns the total number of South Africans currently infected. Although, through annual sampling, the country has a fairly good estimate of the HIV prevalence rate among pregnant women (24,5 per cent), the rate among the population at large is based on modelling and is therefore more suspect. The figure quoted for the total number of South Africans living with HIV / AIDS is 4,7 million or 11 per cent of the population as a whole. The predicted figure in 2010 ranges from six to eight million. The second uncertainty relates to the long-term socioeconomic impact of HIV / AIDS. Nobody really knows how much society or the economy is going to be affected; but the change could be substantial and surprising. The third uncertainty – and most critical of all – is how the nation in the short term is going to respond to the challenge posed by the epidemic.

Basically, there are three scenarios. The first one is "Denial" where the nation continues to behave as though the epidemic does not exist. Eventually, the AIDS deaths rise to a level where the scenario can no longer be sustained; but meanwhile valuable time for combating HIV is lost. The second scenario is "Business as Usual". The HIV/AIDS epidemic is acknowledged as a threat, but it is not considered an important priority. Public attention is drawn to the disease whenever there is a special day or conference. Otherwise life goes on pretty much as usual, except that the number of young, gifted and dead rise remorselessly. The third scenario is "Total Onslaught" where the government, captains of industry and other influential leaders jointly declare war on the virus. It receives the highest priority in terms of money, manpower and other resources. The nation rises to the occasion with the same resolve as it would if it were invaded by a human enemy to be repelled at all costs. Victory is the only thought on everybody's mind.

The options comprise the range of actions available to government, the private sector and civil society generally. Quite simply, it boils down to where the disease stands in the national list of priorities. Will it be elevated to the No. 1 issue or will it remain a middle-order item? The kind of actions which will signify an increase in national emphasis on the epidemic are the implementation of proper HIV/AIDS prevention programmes in every primary and secondary school, university and technikon as well as on the shop floor; the availability of a voluntary counselling and testing facility to all citizens, accompanied by a wellness programme for those that test positive, and counselling for those that test negative to stay that way; the free issue of drugs to stop mother-to-child transmission; the establishment of a network of STD clinics so that people can get themselves regularly checked out and, if necessary, treated;

a support system to care for the orphans; and the intensification of the search for a vaccine. Indeed, vaccines and cures at this stage are very much wild cards. If they come about, fantastic! But don't count on them for planning purposes.

You might say that this list breaks a fundamental rule of the game, which is affordability. The answer is that each community does as much as it can on each of these fronts within the realms of affordability. Obviously, therefore, the response of drug companies is crucial. Will they cut the prices of HIV/AIDS therapies to a level where they can reach the masses? And will they assist in setting up the infrastructure necessary to administer the therapies? The other serious option is the one that can be exercised by the individual in terms of protecting his or her own body. HIV is not an airborne disease like flu: in the majority of cases of HIV transmission, it requires a conscious decision on the part of the individual to indulge in risky behaviour. The exceptions are rape, child abuse, mother-to-child transmission, blood transfusions and accidental contact involving blood. Nevertheless, as the first "A" of AIDS spells out, it is almost always *acquired*. Hence, the degree to which individuals are prepared to change their sexual habits becomes a crucial variable in how the epidemic finally pans out. And the best way to change behaviour in youngsters is to offer them options to minimise the risk of infection, rather than issue them with a specific set of instructions to do so. They need to feel that they are in control and free to choose.

So let's get up close and personal. Suppose you're lecturing your young daughter about the birds and the bees. The matrix comes in very handy. The rule of the game is simple: unprotected sex runs the risk of HIV. She can't change that – it's a biological rule, *not* a parental rule. Like crossing a rifle range when shooting is in progress, there are inherent dangers. The key uncertainty is not whether but when, where and by whom she is first going to be propositioned to have sex. The scenarios are "no"; "yes" with no consequences and "yes" with consequences. Her options are to abstain with no risk of transmission; have protected sex which reduces the chances of transmission; or just do it which carries a big health warning. You love her and in no way wish to diminish her joys of discovering love and sex for herself. Moreover, no-one else has the same interest in protecting her body as she does. She is in control, and thus has every right to choose from amongst the three options. Eventually, when she settles down with a partner she trusts, she can choose differently. Nevertheless, in the meantime if you were her, your decision would be to abstain, abstain, abstain, but in a *sexual emergency* insist on a condom. And if any sugar daddy should approach her with predatory intentions, here's a whistle for her to blow. You'll come running to rescue her from his clutches!

Now we must revert to the national situation and examine the fourth quadrant of the matrix on page 127. It is one big question mark. Who knows what decisions will be taken and which scenarios will materialise? We don't. But the future is not, as they say in the classics, "in the lap of the gods". It will be determined by individual South Africans.

Cinderella Rockefeller

Imagine you are Cinderella – the poor sister. But there is no grand ball to dress up for, no glass slipper to be lost, no prince to discover it and seek whom it fits. Yet you are struck with this burning ambition to overtake your ugly sisters and leave them breathing in your dust. What do you do? The answer for today's confident modern maiden is: open up your own business. What advice can the matrix give you so that one day you're as rich as Rockefeller?

The first rule of the game surrounds the eight characteristics of being world class. Given globalisation, no matter how small you are, you will probably be facing world-class competition – if not in the form of a company like Coca-Cola, then in the form of a franchise like McDonald's. So you have to shape up or ship out. Therefore the No. 1 characteristic is passion. You must choose something you're passionate about because you're probably better at pursuing your passion than doing other things. The question is how you turn that passion into a commercial opportunity. Once you've settled on a line of business, focus is the second characteristic and being different or unique in some way is the third. Collecting a team of like-minded talented young people, usually old school chums, around you is the fourth characteristic and studying global practice is the fifth. The sixth is never to give up on innovation of your product or service, while the seventh is to have an in-built

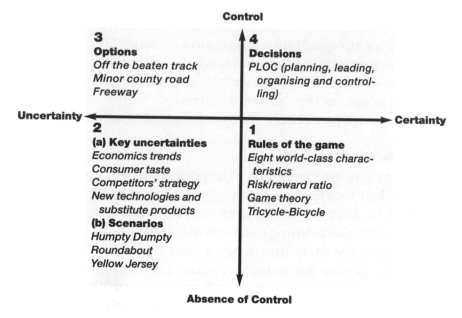

radar system picking up on opportunities and threats. Last but by no means least – and remembering all we said earlier – you have to be ethical in all senses of the word and to all stakeholders.

The second rule of the game concerns the potential risks and rewards associated with the business you've selected. If you recall our pleasure and pain curve, you have to ask yourself what kind of loss you can stomach should things go wrong. Then you have to tailor-make your start-up cost so that it does not exceed your limit, or find others to share the risk with you before you go ahead. In the latter case, it's better to go for venture capital in the form of equity rather than debt. A wonderful initiative in America is the Tuesday Forum where, on the first Tuesday of every month, venture capital seekers and providers meet at a suitable venue to matchmake. While you're raising capital you need to remember that statistically the first few businesses are usually failures before you hit the right button; thus the need to keep some funds in reserve to try again.

The third rule of the game relates to game theory which we've already explained. What are other competitors likely to do when you enter the market and how can you counter their response?

For the fourth rule, remember the old adage "don't run before you can walk" and transfer it to the world of cycling. It becomes "don't graduate to two wheels before you've learnt to ride on three". A tricycle has three wheels positioned in a triangular configuration designed for maximum stability in order to supply balance for a beginner. In the case of a first-time entrepreneur, the front wheel represents the strategy which gives direction to a business. The two back wheels are the operating efficiencies and financial controls which provide stability to ensure that the business is sustainable. However, as the business grows, so the need becomes apparent for the original founder to back off from personally doing everything on the ground and become a manager of other people doing these tasks. This involves a different set of skills and the acceptance of a hierarchy, which causes the organisation to shift from a horizontal to a vertical structure. The equivalent is graduating from a tricycle to a bicycle where the front wheel is still strategy and the back wheel is a combination of operational and financial systems required to manage the business. The entrepreneur is now the manager perched on the elevated seat striving to keep the bicycle balanced as it rounds bends and jumps on bumps in the road. The cycling analogy explains why so many start-ups fail. Either one of the wheels of the tricycle is missing to start with, causing it to overturn; or the entrepreneur is like the kid who graduates too fast to the bicycle stage, then takes his hands off the handlebars and says "look, Ma, no hands" as he heads into the bush!

The key uncertainties awaiting your new-born business are daunting. The first is the immediate future of the economy, and specifically your market, after you've opened your doors. We're afraid to say that good timing is more a matter of luck than anything else, because market turning-points are usually unpredictable. Then there's the question of customer taste. They say there's no accounting for taste and it's fickle at the best of times: one moment you're in fashion, the next you're not. So you continuously need something new up your sleeve. If that's not enough, competitors can pull surprising moves out of the hat just when you've settled down; and new technologies can come along which make your product obsolete by offering cheaper or better substitutes. All these uncertainties demonstrate the need for a radar system to detect incoming missiles!

What are the scenarios for your business? Basically three. The first is "Humpty Dumpty". Your business falls off the wall fairly early on and neither you, nor your friends, nor your bankers can put it back together again. The second scenario is "Roundabout". Your business survives but it never gets beyond the survivalist stage either because you are not steering your tricycle properly on account of having no strategy; or because your back wheels aren't balanced and you lack the combination of operational efficiency and financial control. The third scenario is "Yellow Jersey" which implies long-term success, seeing that this is the jersey that the ultimate winner of the Tour de France cycling race wears as he collects his prize. You don't have to win individual stages but the race overall. The same applies in business: rather than focusing on short-term increases in market share or the quarterly financial results, the entrepreneur with the yellow jersey aims to grow shareholder value in the long term. Endurance – rather than the ability to make short sprints – is what really counts.

Bearing in mind these scenarios, we now move on to the top half of the matrix to examine the options that you can choose between. The first is to go off the beaten track and open up an entirely original business. However, you need an organisation behind you as sturdy as a mountain bike to withstand all the ridges, rocks and ditches presenting themselves en route. The second option is to take a minor country road and start a more conventional business which basically caters for the local market. There will still be the odd pothole and corrugation in the road to give you an occasional shock. But now you have to be wary of other traffic and in particular other entrepreneurial cyclists who may try to overtake you as you reach your business destination. The third option is to cycle up on to the freeway, advertise yourself on the Internet and carve out a global niche. The caution you have to exercise here is to stay away from freeways which can only be used by vehicles of the four-wheel kind, namely bigger businesses that can achieve greater economies of scale than you can. Moreover, the bicycles which are likely to pass you now are the ultra-light racing ones ridden by ultra-fit guys in lycra bodysuits and streamlined helmets. Standards are much higher in the international arena!

At this point, you make your selection; and we can't make it for you. But as we've said all along, it's one thing to make a decision and quite another to get the result. Here, the PLOC principle comes into play – planning, leading, organising and controlling. The plan is the chain of decisions and the resources required to turn the idea into a commercial reality. Leadership is what you have to display to get all your troops facing in the right direction and to persuade those not under your command but nevertheless vital for the success of the project, like financiers and suppliers, to give you their whole-hearted support. Organisation and control are the two back wheels of the tricycle. When you get more experienced, they are combined in the back wheel of your bicycle. They ensure that your business remains balanced even when you hit a rough patch or the wind blows straight into your face.

So, good luck, Cinderella! Maybe you'll lure a prince into matrimony one day because you're worth a fortune. Then you'll live happily ever after in a castle you purchased off the Internet.

Crouching Tiger, Winning Fox

Time flies like the wind: fruit flies like bananas! We hope time has flown for you; and you have had as much fun reading this book as we have had in writing it. We have touched many bases; unashamedly mixed our metaphors such as Tiger crouching over his putt as a winning fox; and produced our own miniseries of Apollo 13. With all the means at our disposal, we have tried to convince you to become a resourceful fox. We want you to be as bold and quick-witted as the fox which, when captured the other day by a hound at a hunt, dragged the hound into a nearby lake in the hope of getting him to let go. A huntsman came to the rescue of both animals, and they lived to fight another day. The huntsman bowed to the fox in respect as it disappeared through the hedge.

Even as you set yourself BHAGs (big, hairy, audacious goals), you often need the nimbleness and flexibility of mind to switch to Plan B to make them happen. Our matrix hopefully prepares you for the unexpected as well as those parts of your life which resemble a roller-coaster ride – when you feel there are powerful forces that are outside your control taking you up to the crest, keeping you hovering in suspense for a few heart-stopping moments before sending you careering down the other side. There are always things you *can* do – like holding on tightly in this case and screaming if you must!

Charles Kingsley made the following remark in his enchanting tale about a young chimney sweep called Tom who joined the Water Babies in the stream: "The most wonderful and the strongest things in the world, you know, are just the things which no one can see." He furnished "life" as an example in that it makes you grow, move and think – and yet you can't see it. Kingsley's quote is as true today as it was in 1863 when he wrote it. Accordingly, you will have noticed how much emphasis we have laid on obeying the invisible, unwritten rules of the game if you want to succeed. Breaking the rules sounds exciting when you're young and naturally rebellious. But it doesn't lead to progress except when the rules are somehow flawed in the first place.

Hence, it is worth following in the footsteps of Mrs Doasyouwouldbedoneby who personified the rules of being a good fairy and gently taught Tom to obey them. Otherwise, you may suffer the dismal fate of the nation of Doasyoulikes who broke every rule in the book and ended up with extinction.

There's a Jewish expression which embodies a similar outlook on life as Kingsley's: you can divide the people in this world into those who would hide you in their loft and those who wouldn't. The selfless and the rest.

On a different note, the film *American Beauty* demonstrated that dysfunctional families are *the* invisible rule of the game in Suburbia; and we should be thankful for the odd moment of peace and tranquillity. So much for progress in the real world. But then foxes do accept that we live in a state of imperfection, and we must make the best out of it.

We also want you to be curious like a fox. It's okay: curiosity only killed the cat. Foxes go through open doors to see what's on the other side; but their nose is twitching and they are ready to turn tail if the adventure becomes too exciting. Opportunistic on the one hand, they are survivalists at heart on the other: remember what we said about keeping opposites in mind. An immensely rich and eminent fox was once asked whether he preferred diamonds or gold. His response was diamonds because woman's vanity would outlast man's greed: diamonds *are* forever! Foxes are neither too vain nor too greedy. They know that vanity dulls the keenness of their senses; and greed distorts their power of reasoning. The same fox commented once that real wealth was acquired through owning, not working. With this in mind, we put in the piece on owning and running a small business because, you never know, you might hit the jackpot and become supersonically rich yourself. The terms "foxy" and "entrepreneurial" are pretty much interchangeable. Yet, you will recall that we talked a lot about values. Social foxes who make a difference in other people's lives are needed just as much as business foxes in this world. Our matrix is as applicable to an NGO striving to do its charitable thing as it is to a company trying to deliver value to its shareholders.

Foxes are trusting creatures, especially of their own kith and kin. However, they have a healthy scepticism of hedgehogs and statistics. In the latter regard, a foxy environmentalist recently quipped that 87 per cent of all statistics are made up on the spur of the moment! This leads us to two themes we have consistently pursued throughout the book: (1) you only get at the truth by discarding all the falsehoods along the way and (2) you only know what you do control when you have learnt about the things that you don't control. We could have called the book *The Heresies of Hedgehogs* and then gone on to prove that the mind of a fox is superior to that of a hedgehog. It would have borne out the first principle! Rather, though, we have followed the injunction of Brother William of Baskerville, who said in Umberto Eco's *The Name of the Rose*: "Perhaps the mission of those who love mankind is to make people laugh at the truth, *to make truth laugh*, because the only truth lies in learning to free ourselves from insane passion for the truth." Anyway, history reveals that a fraction of "heretics" like Copernicus and Galileo are proved right in the long run.

Thus, we readily admit that our matrix is not a perfect, all-inclusive answer to how you should handle the future. But it is a sufficiently close reflection of the way we *naturally* think for us to believe that it serves a useful purpose. In other words, we have tried to make explicit the internal thought processes we instinctively go through when facing a challenging situation. We've also tried to give the technique of scenario planning a shot in the arm by putting it in

139

its proper context in the chain of reasoning that leads to a good decision. We are sure that one day scenario planning will take its rightful place alongside strategic planning as an essential management tool. Common sense dictates it in a world of accelerating change and increasing discontinuity. Moreover, although we've been pretty negative about hedgehogs throughout this book, they have every right to exist and a society without them would be the poorer for their absence. So we are not asking the whole world to become foxes. After all, hedgehogs with a penchant for stability and order offset the slightly anarchical tendencies of foxes.

However, we would suggest that it is better by far to think like a fox, particularly in these uncertain times. It is not that Peter Drucker's concept of management by objectives – the very foundation of American management thinking for the last half of the previous century – is wrong. It is incomplete. When the future resembled the past as it did in the 1950s and 1960s and less so in the 1970s and 1980s, you could set objectives and measure your performance against those objectives. But now we live in a world where millions, or maybe billions, of people have instantaneous access to information and, more importantly, breaking news. When changes happen, particularly in markets, they can be of such a magnitude that they turn all the assumptions on which you have based your objectives upside down – just like that. Management by objectives does not allow for this, as it is firmly located in our fourth quadrant: get experts in to analyse the uncertainty out of the future and assume that you have total control to achieve the objectives specified. Alas, things aren't so neat now and you simply cannot operate like that anymore. In the current environment, strategic thinking must be seen less as a process of gazing into a crystal ball to determine your long-term future and more as a way of preparing yourself for any eventuality that may come your way. Flexibility in thinking is the important outcome. However, a sensitivity to what should remain the same and you should be steadfast about is also crucial. Foxes strive to find the right balance. Regular visits to all four quadrants of our matrix are therefore essential to ensure that you have set the most appropriate objectives in the first place and that you review them in a logical manner as the fog enveloping the future clears.

And you can be wrong! Then at least you have the means to analyse why you went wrong. It could be that you misidentified a rule of the game; or you didn't capture a key uncertainty or surprise; or you bet on the wrong scenario. Or even that you implemented the decision wrong. The matrix should never be put in the bottom drawer of the desk like a strategic plan. It is a compass to negotiate your way through the fog and make course corrections as necessary.

Do you recall Winnie-the-Pooh, A. A. Milne's Bear of Very Little Brain? He felt that "a Thing which seemed very Thingish inside you is quite different when it gets out into the open and has other people looking at it". Scenario planners want to bring our unconscious prejudices to the surface so that we can acknowledge them and look at the forces driving the world in an unvarnished way. The masters of the scenario game – Herman Kahn, Pierre Wack, Ted Newland, Peter Schwartz and Edouard Parker – all leave you with a feeling that, by removing the filters, they have opened up a brand new world of possibilities. You'll get the same feeling from reading *The Tipping Point* by Malcolm Gladwell in which he explains how little things can make a big difference. A fox after our own hearts! Once you delve into his book, you'll never view epidemics in the same light again. Well, we want our matrix to be contagious too so that it assists people to reperceive the future in a way that works better for them.

The proof is in the pudding. We've tried the matrix out in seminars that we have facilitated and it has worked like a charm. It brings fresh angles to the debate around the table. More importantly, it brings people from disparate backgrounds together – managers, union representatives, public servants, local community leaders, etc. – and binds them more closely to one another because they are all involved in formulating the content of the matrix. The spontaneity and interaction of the group as each person builds on the ideas of others means that the final picture cannot be predicted in advance. Indeed, we recommend minimal preparation in advance of a scenario planning session. Moreover, at the end of it all, no-one is under any illusion about the real rules of the game governing the activity in which he or she is a participant. This makes subsequent negotiations easier because they will take place within a common framework of understanding.

Laird Hamilton is still alive today because he is familiar with the matrix. He is the king of big wave surfing and knows just how many factors are completely beyond his control in heavy seas. Yet he has revolutionised surfing with two modifications within his control: putting straps on the board to bind the feet and being towed by a jet ski instead of paddling to catch the waves initially. In the extremest of extreme sports where waves can reach the monstrous height of ten metres, he survives because he is smart.

But try the matrix for yourself. Try it in your personal life when you next have to make a difficult decision about people, money or a job. Try it when considering the opening up of your own business. Try it in your company at your next annual strategic get-together.

And may the fox be with you!

Postscript

Whatever path the future takes, the "rich old millions" are going to spend more time in Quadrant 2 of our matrix (where things are uncertain and beyond their control) and less time in Quadrant 4 (where things are certain and under their thumb). Hence the relevance of our book: making people think more like foxes and less like hedgehogs.

The signs of looming trouble have been there, now that our ability to destroy ourselves far outstrips our ability to preserve ourselves. Moreover, the idea that mutually assured destruction acts as a deterrent is as obsolete as the two-superpower model for which it was devised. Something more constructive has to replace it.

In a book published in 1992 with the title *The New Century**, one of us wrote the following: "Against that [the containment of any future war through joint action by America and Russia] the odds of a nuclear exchange are increasing as the knowledge of producing ballistic missiles and nuclear warheads disseminates through the Third World (the nuclear risk also applies to any conflict between Pakistan and India over disputed territory on their borders).

"The growth of fundamentalist Islam poses a serious challenge to Western lifestyles and values. This in itself is not a geopolitical problem. It only becomes one if attempts are made by zealots to impose Islam on countries wishing to pursue other paths of development. The attractions to the 'poor young billions' of a religion based on the strict code of the Koran are obvious. It anchors their existence in spiritual certainties when all is flux around them; it gives a clear sense of purpose in a world that for many has no meaning

*Clem Sunter, *The New Century* (p. 129), published by Human & Rousseau / Tafelberg, Cape Town, 1992.

whatsoever; and it abhors materialism, a quality the poor do not possess anyway through force of circumstance. The Middle East, Pakistan, the southern republics of the former Soviet Union and northern Africa are all falling under the spell of fundamentalist Islam. That is a formidable area of influence. How much further it will spread and at what rate is unknown. Equally unknown is whether the spreading of an idea will degenerate into a war of beliefs. A nuclear *jihad* is not out of the question. Fundamentalist Islam is a wild card with the ability to alter the balance of power in important parts of the world."

Chilling stuff. If there is a nuclear exchange, where does the radioactive fall-out caused by the detonation of the bombs end up? For example, the fall-out from the accident at the Chernobyl nuclear power plant reached as far up as Scandinavia. In times like these, you have to play scenarios to capture all the possible consequences.We cannot choose when we are born and – for most of us – when we die. Nevertheless, we can choose *how* we live in the epoch allotted to us. Let us choose, each in our own way, to work towards a Friendly Planet and avert such desperate consequences.